TABLE OF CONTENTS

D0289268

TABLE OF CONTENTS

GAMBLE TO WIN ROULETTE

R. D. Ellison

A Lyle Stuart Book
Kensington Publishing Corporation
www.kensingtonbooks.com

Lyle Stuart books are published by

Kensington Publishing Corp.
850 Third Avenue
New York, NY 10022

© 2002 R.D. Ellison

All Kensington titles, imprints, and distributed lines are available at special quantity discounts for bulk purchases for sales promotions, premiums, fund raising, educational, or institutional use. Special book excerpts or customized printings can also be created to fit specific needs. For details, write or phone the office of the Kensington special sales manager: Kensington Publishing Corp., 850 Third Avenue, New York, NY 10022, attn: Special Sales Department, phone 1-800-221-2647.

Lyle Stuart is a trademark of Kensington Publishing Corp.

First printing April 2002

10 9 8 7 6 5 4 3 2 1

Printed in the United States of America

Library of Congress Control Number 2001099891

ISBN: 0-8184-0627-5

TABLE OF CONTENTS

PART III: STRATEGIES

TABLE OF CONTENTS

TABLE OF CONTENTS

TABLE OF CONTENTS

PART V: PUTTING IT ALL TOGETHER

PREFACE

Throughout modern history, the consensus among gaming experts was that no system or strategy could aspire to overcome the 5.26% house edge at American roulette. The math, they have always said, is unassailable.

This, R. D. Ellison's third book, has changed that. His *3Q/A Reverse Select* strategy has been tested against over 7,000 roulette spins (that represent 357 live sessions) printed in Frank Scoblete's *Spin Roulette Gold,* published by Bonus Books. In that study, the win rate of the 3Q/A completely eliminated the effects of the house edge, offering in its stead an overall statistical advantage of 7.22% *to the player.*

Another study against Erick St. Germain's *Roulette System Tester* resulted in an even greater mathematical edge for the player. And that edge was yet again exceeded in other trials. Since the two reference books mentioned are still in print, all the results have been, and can be, independently verified.

These verification methods were chosen because the 3Q/A procedure is not adaptable to computer simulations, since the table has to be 'qualified' before the strategy variation can be chosen, and play can begin.

While the samplings are too small to be statistically absolute, never before has a roulette strategy withstood such a rigorous test. *Gamble to Win Roulette* has accomplished what was previously believed impossible: to offer a strategy that maintains a consistent mathematical player advantage over American roulette.

INTRODUCTION

As I walked past a roulette table in Trump Plaza, I couldn't help but notice the coverage on number 17. The chips were stacked eighteen inches high on that number, and I could tell—from the stripes in the stack of chips—that all of the players at the table had contributed to the pile.

Now, this matter of stacking is a gray area, because the rules for how high you can go will vary from one casino to the next. It may even vary from one roulette pit to the next in the same casino. On the one hand, casino management appreciates a good crowd pleaser when an opportunity presents itself, but they also want to avoid disputes over who bet what, if the stack should fall. In this case, no one had objected.

The dealer set the ball loose in the spinning wheel, and up popped a number that didn't even resemble a 17. He took care in disassembling the pile of losing chips, but when he lifted the dolly, the players feverishly re-created the pile.

This ritual continued for several more spins, but the elusive number 17 never showed. Suddenly, all the players abandoned the table en masse, their compulsive bets having tapped them dry. The once-lively table was now vacant.

I started to walk away, but then noticed an older woman—dressed like a bag lady—on the opposite side of the table from where I stood. She approached the empty table, set down her bags, and took a seat. To my surprise, she put five white chips on the 17. Captivated by her stupidity, I stuck around to see her bet go down. It didn't. The 17 won.

Dressed as she was, I was sure she'd take the money and run. Instead, she repeated her five-chip bet on the 17, and added some multiple-chip coverage to a few of the lower numbers, using the chips she'd just won. Number 5 won, which she covered. She was now over $300 ahead from two spins that had taken place in about two minutes. The dealer had to make part of the new payoff with reds and greens, because she had tapped *him* out of the whites he had been using to pay her.

I looked around. No one was watching but me. I've seen a lot of amazing things in casinos, but this was beyond amazing. And yet, she was just warming up.

The woman left the table after about ten spins, roughly $900 ahead. She had caught the 17 three times, along with quite a few other numbers.

To this day, I still wonder who she was, and how she did that. Might be a good candidate for *Unsolved Mysteries*.

PART I

THE BASICS

1

A NUMBERS GAME

Welcome to the world of selective wagering, where casino games are used as vehicles for generating and leveraging income. Here, you will learn how to capitalize upon your prowess as an interpreter of random numerical events.

Playing casino games effectively is nothing more than a numbers game. Your goal is to outsmart the table by anticipating the next number. This doesn't sound so hard when one considers that your rival has no cognitive skills with which to thwart your efforts, but there are compensating factors that it *does* possess. And these can present a mean challenge.

To acquire the requisite skill to meet this challenge, you will need to understand probabilities, trends, risk management, and how to regulate the monetary flow.

But those are extensions of the base qualities I consider to be most important. When you whittle away the excess, perhaps the main ingredient you will need is *patience*. This is the one you can't do without.

Beyond that, you will need to cultivate discipline, strategy, and precision technique. And, to be mentally prepared for the full range of outcomes every time you play.

If you can handle that, you may find that this book offers the best operating guidelines that are currently available for waging commercial warfare against the casinos.

A PORTFOLIO OF PLAYS

If you've read the Preface, you should be somewhat aware that the centerpiece strategy of this book is referred to as the *3Q/A Reverse Select,* and, that in comprehensive trials, this has been proven to yield a decisive statistical advantage to the player. So why don't we peel off the fat and get to it? We don't need to know anything else, right?

I'm not trying to make you feel bad, but anyone who agrees with the logic of those last two questions did not connect with the content of the preceding page: *patience.* That is the key. That is the first thing that has to be learned, and it must be learned well.

Everything that precedes the information you desire has a purpose. Virtually every bit of it will be needed at points along the way. Some of it may be thrown out, but it must be understood before it is discarded.

For example, you have to know the rules of the game, how big a bankroll you need, and when a session should start and end. You must understand table limits and other restrictions, including some that are purely psychological, yet unavoidable. You need to know what you're getting into, because the time for hesitation or doubt is *not* when your money is on the line.

The 3Q/A isn't the only strategy offered in this book. There are others that some readers may prefer as their specialties. But more importantly, it's best to avoid a one-dimensional approach. What you want is a portfolio of plays, so you can capitalize on all types of table patterns.

Unless, you would prefer death by monotony.

AN INTERPRETATION OF THE LAW OF AVERAGES

Amongst gaming authors, and people associated with the subject matter, this so-called *Law of Averages* is something of a political hot potato. Most of these experts say that every decision at a casino table game is independent of all those that preceded it. The tables have no memory. Therefore, to claim that a number is "due" is pure hogwaller.

But is it? Their argument sounds logical, but if what they said was absolutely true, it would be possible for a given roulette table, for example, to never even once produce the number 5 in twenty million consecutive spins. Now, do you really think that would ever happen?

Unless the wheel was biased, there is *no chance* that *could* happen. Sooner or later, the number 5 will come up. Remember, we're talking about millions of table results, a one-in-38 chance, and a level playing field.

What this tells us, is that within any (sustained) numerical sequence, events with equal probabilities will move toward a state of parity with the others. That is to say, *there is ongoing statistical pressure on every playable number to appear within a given timeframe.*

In his book, *Can You Win,* Mike Orkin, who has a Ph.D. in Statistics from the University of California, Berkeley, seemed to concur with this when he wrote:

In repeated, independent trials of the same experiment, the observed fraction of occurrences of an event eventually approaches its theoretical probability.

But that doesn't mean an event is 'due.' There's another force at work here, which is often overlooked: Trends. Flukes, which seem to possess a will of their own and yet are simply random occurrences. Regarding these, there is scant information in many books, despite the fact that they are at the very heart of professional gambling.

Those experts who say that the *Law of Averages* is a load of crud may take comfort in the fact that the Vegas betting favorite won the Superbowl nine out of the last ten games (1992–2001). Or, that no favorite has won the Kentucky Derby in the last 20 years or so. Not much averaging going on there!

In spite of the evidence presented above, those examples do not disprove the Law of Averages. Flukes happen. Not just in the casinos, but also in everyday life. Most people don't pay much attention to the everyday variety, though, for these types seldom involve monetary swings of fortune. When money is on the line, one is much more likely to notice!

The Law of Averages does indeed exist. And so do Trends. The two are constantly at odds with each other, in such a way that they often cancel each other out. If you are seeking success at the tables, you must believe in both. You must understand that they will work for and against you. You must be aware of their influence when putting down your bets.

Personally, I appreciate the existence of this numerical law. It is of some comfort to know that the probabilities tend to move toward a state of balance. Without knowing that, I would feel lost most of the time. It would be much more difficult for me to make an intuitive projection of the outcome.

What it comes down to, is that in affairs of chance, it's only a matter of time before the *Law of Averages* begins to intercede and impose its will. Because, behind this ubiquitous law, there is a statistical imperative:

Given time, events will seek their proper place within their assigned probabilities.

Knowing this, is what helps guide me to the best wagering choice at the tables.

THE PATIENCE IMPERATIVE

Impatience is the enemy.

—a New York Investment firm

Years ago, I remember seeing a magazine advertisement where David Niven was saying "I hate to wait." At the time, his message sounded a bit arrogant. The big movie star wants special treatment. But then I realized that I'm not overly fond of waiting, myself. My disdain for the act of waiting is so strong, in fact, that I would gladly repeat those very words on national television, for the price of a stick of gum!

And when you look at it analytically, waiting is more than just an inconvenience. It's down time. A period when you are forced to be unproductive. Part of what irritates me about waiting is the frustration of being prevented from moving forward, when I'm a moving-forward kind of guy. There are times, however, when waiting is the only way to achieve the goal of being the most productive you can be.

It is human nature to want simplicity, fast results, and easy money. But the things in life that mean the most, take time and effort to acquire.

There *is* a human characteristic which tends to separate the winners (in casinos) from the losers: Patience.

The message here, is that before you can learn how to Win, you must first learn how to Not Lose. And the surest path to both is to have the patience of a saint, all the time, every day, every session, and with every bet you make.

Think about that, next time you're sitting there wondering why you're not winning more often!

ROULETTE RENAISSANCE?

Recently, in a correspondence from a friend in Europe, I was asked for my thoughts on the possibility of what he termed as a *Roulette Renaissance.*

At the time, it sounded a bit implausible to me. A rebirth or revival of roulette? For whom: the casinos, or the players? Either way, I see problems. If it's for the casinos, that means the players will lose that much more. And if it's for the players, the casinos will surely take measures to combat this assault upon their divine right to make money hand over fist.

In spite of the above, I'm having trouble dismissing the idea, particularly in light of my awareness of the new concepts that are introduced in this book. And so I must conclude that a renaissance *is* possible for a select few. But who among all the players of the world will be chosen?

I'd like to think that every reader of this book will be part of this era of player-side supremacy, but I know only too well the odds against it. Because, as that friend once pointed out to me, readers of gaming books are an impatient lot. Casino gaming for many of them is a last resort in their quest for greatness. They turn to it only after having failed in pursuit of finding a cure for cancer, or inventing a perpetual motion machine.

So, the real question is not who will be chosen, but rather, who will do what's necessary to make it happen? Every reader of this book has the potential to be part of this renaissance, if he learns the subject matter inside out, and resolves to meet, head on, the requirements of this endeavor.

Roulette Renaissance?

Difficult, but not impossible.

2

THE POWERS THAT BE

*Nobody **gives** you power, boy. Real power is something you* ***take!***

—Jock Ewing to Bobby,
from TV drama *Dallas*

In any competitive trial, it is imperative that one understands the strengths and weaknesses of his adversary. What is the worst he can do to you? What is the worst you can do to him? Like any capable general engaged in battle, one should be prepared for the full spectrum of strategic possibilities.

This applies especially in casino gaming, for your opponent has accumulated a track record that is worthy of deep admiration. One can learn from success of that magnitude.

To better understand why the casinos are so successful, one needs to study the point of view of *the powers that be.* What are all the little tricks they use to separate you from your money? Which ones are the most effective, and how are they interwoven so as to achieve such laudable results?

In other words, the best way to beat the casino—when you're at the tables—is to *think like a casino,* and put your money at risk in much the same way as they do!

9

BEHIND THE FACADE

We haven't done our job until the customer's last check has bounced.

—a former owner of Binion's Horseshoe

Casinos by their very nature are painstakingly designed to be the ultimate in lavish surroundings, glitter, hospitality and comfort. If there is not a palpable feel of excitement in the air, and if you're not convinced that you can find your fortune within those walls, then somebody isn't doing their job. Casino management, I should think, is due for a shakedown.

Every member of the casino staff is so nice; so friendly. They make you feel like you're an honored guest. They pamper you and cater to your every whim. But as you're leaving, you might notice that you're exiting with much less money than when you arrived. Now that's odd! During the course of your stay, you thought you were winning. But what seemed to be the perfect escape from the harsh realities of life came with a price tag after all. Just like all those other harsh realities.

But how did they do that? What buttons did they push to get you to spend all that money?

Casino entrapment, as we might call it, has over the years been studied, perfected, and refined to a science. The casinos are not guessing when they separate you from your money. They are a highly tuned machine that executes its craft with the cold precision and efficiency of a supercomputer.

It all *seems* so warm, inviting, and appealing. But behind the façade, it's all smoke and mirrors.

Two of the newest casino megaresorts in Las Vegas cost no less than $1.5 billion to build (Bellagio, $1.6B; Venetian, $1.5B). That's a lot of money, wouldn't you say? Do you suppose they'll ever recoup such a huge investment?

Of course, those two properties command fairly good prices for their hotel rooms (over $100 a night; much more during peak periods), and both resorts have over 3000 rooms. But that's not where the real money is made.

Before getting into the casino business, Donald Trump once gathered some information about the profitability of Hilton hotels, and discovered that two of Hilton's 150 hotels accounted for nearly 40% of the company's net profits! Those two were located in Las Vegas, and had casinos attached. The magic link! Soon after that, Mr. Trump decided to enter the casino business.

So while the hotel room rates help casino resorts maintain a steady income, the casino games are what push their profits up to the skies.

So how is it that casinos are such a good investment? What is it that makes them so outrageously successful? It all comes down to three Cs and an H: *Cocooning, Compulsion, Continuum,* and of course, *House Edge.*

The first of these, *Cocooning,* comes in the form of a warm, exciting and friendly environment that keeps you detached from the outside world. This is accomplished by having no windows in a gaming area that otherwise would have a spectacular ocean view (as in Atlantic City); ensuring there are no clocks in the gaming area (so you will lose track of time); making you use gaming chips (that help you lose a sense of all that money you're spending), and hiring beautiful, sexy cocktail waitresses that offer you free drinks. There are women in the world to whom a man can say *no. . .*but as a rule, not these!

These are just a few of the tricks that comprise the cocooning effect, but the other three are the biggies:

Compulsion, continuum, and house edge. These are the ones you should fear the most. Before visiting a casino, you should know what they are, and what they do.

COMPULSION

Remember, the House doesn't beat a player. It merely gives him the opportunity to beat himself.

—Nick 'the Greek' Dandalos

Compulsion is defined in the American Heritage Dictionary as *an irresistable impulse to act, regardless the rationality of the motivation.*

The above definition has been abridged to reflect only the part that is relevant for this context. In casino gaming, it describes those adverse personality traits the casinos attempt to coax out of you: hedonism and greed.

Compulsion is a tough adversary, because fighting it involves fighting yourself! Or, more specifically, your natural inclinations. Even seasoned pros can succumb to this beast, for although they have to some degree learned to suppress it, it's always lurking in the shadows. It's like a time bomb, ticking away. And then, after it explodes, the looters come, and pick you clean. But don't blame them. They're just doing their job.

It is only natural, when losing, to find yourself edging toward a state of panic. How are you going to absolve the losses you just incurred? You're upset, because somebody just took your money away; money that was very precious to you.

Perhaps now (after eight straight losses) is the time to *load up* and get it all back with one large, well-timed bet.

Seems, at the time, like a pretty good plan.

This is what goes through one's mind. It's just part of being human. The casinos know it. They wait for it. It's the reason for their success. Watching their guests self-destruct before their eyes is part of their daily routine.

Want to hear the outcome of that large, well-timed bet? There are but three possibilities:

1) The player reached into his pocket and realized that he was tapped out. The bet was planned but never made.
2) He lost that bet also, which brought his string of losses to nine. (Don't think it can't happen to you.)
3) He won, and was very pleased with himself until the next crisis, when he tried it again, and lost BIG.

Don't be thinking that number three could have worked out. Winning a bet conceived through one's surrender to *compulsion* worsens the problem by validating a terrible habit. When allowed to flourish, that habit will devolve into self-deception that will take you in one direction—which is the opposite of *Up*.

Would you believe, *Compulsion* also works against you when you're winning! When things go well at the tables, one tends to feel invincible. This is your big moment! As the wheel spins, you imagine the outcome of your glorious night in the casino, when you could do no wrong. But then the ball comes to rest, and the dealer announces *"Number 36, red."*

Oh, man, how could that happen? You were on a roll. There was no way you could lose. But it happened, and so, the beautiful dream went down in flames.

"He shouldn't have pressed his luck," whispered one of the players at the table to another, who nodded.

That's the trouble with beautiful dreams. Sometimes, if you let reality enter the picture, all that's left is smoke and ash. And that won't even pay your bus fare home.

That's okay. You'll get 'em next time. You've just gotta steer clear of your intrinsic foe, *Compulsion*.

CONTINUUM

The applicable definition of *Continuum* is *a continuous extent or succession that has no arbitrary division.*

Casino games move fast. Decision after decision occurs, and the action never stops. You may have just won a thousand with a bet at the roulette table, but you have no time to savor that victory or plan your next move, for the wheel never stops turning. Do you give up your seat at the table, or temporize with a small bet? This is *Continuum:* an absence of time to respond to the never-ending succession of betting opportunities.

What about the players making smaller bets? They also fall victim because they stay too long. Within minutes, they lose ability to keep pace with the action, and seldom have the sense to quit after a big score, *if* they get that lucky in the first place.

My roulette sessions usually last just a few minutes. By that time, I've sized up the table, and asked myself the all-important question: *Am I winning at this table?* If so, then I should have reached my win goal by that time. If not, then I acknowledge that those table results are not compatible with whatever it is I'm doing, and get on out of there.

That's the way to do it.

Too many players have the nasty habit of playing down to their last chip. The repetition and monotony of ongoing play pulls them in, and turns them all into reckless, irresponsible, mechanical robots that move without thinking.

That is the hypnotic effect of that unconscionable foe that is referred to in this book as *Continuum.*

HOUSE EDGE

The first thing a gambler must do is accept the fact that the House has a clear edge in every casino game.

—Miron Stabinsky, from
Zen and the Art of Casino Gambling

Now we shall take a look at that statistical vampire known as the House Edge. This is one concept you should be clear on, for it is what guarantees the casinos a winning position.

House Edge is the mathematical advantage casinos hold over players, by paying off winning bets for less than what should be paid to *fairly* compensate the risk involved. See, there is a precise statistical probability for every bet you can make in a casino. If the payoffs were aligned perfectly with the probabilities, then in theory the casino could never win in the long run.

The house edge is the unseen foe that never sleeps. It works against you with every bet you make, grinding away your fortunes with persistent malicious intent.

We will look at the game of American roulette to illustrate. This game has 38 playable numbers: 1 through 36, plus 0 and 00. If you place a bet on one of these numbers and win, you'll be paid 35 to 1. But the mathematical probability of winning that bet is 37 ways to lose, and 1 way to win. So, you're paid 35 to 1 for taking a 37 to 1 risk. The difference is the house edge.

At American roulette, that edge works out to 5.26%, which means that the casino earns an average of $5.26 out of every $100 wagered, by virtue of that numerical advantage.

All games are structured to guarantee the house a favorable position in this way. In theory, as long as the casinos keep their games moving, they can do nothing but win, for the numbers will automatically fall in their favor. And that's all it takes to make a successful business.

In Nevada, some casinos advertise a 98% return on their slot machines. What this means, is that for every dollar taken in, an average of 98¢ is returned to the player in the form of wins. How do they make money? Volume. If the casino's take from its slots is five million dollars a day, it will net $100,000. Not a bad day's pay for a game that doesn't even require a dealer.

Figure 1 below shows a simplified listing of the statistical casino advantage for certain casino games. These are arranged in order, with the best bets in the higher positions:

GAME / BET	HOUSE EDGE
Craps: Pass Line bet with double odds	0.60%
Craps: Pass Line bet with single odds	0.80%
MiniBaccarat: Bank bet	1.17%
European Roulette with *En Prison:* Even money bets	1.35%
MiniBaccarat: Player bet	1.36%
Craps: Pass Line or Don't Pass bet (only)	1.41%
Craps: Place bet on the 6 or 8	1.52%
Atlantic City Roulette: Even money bets	2.63%
European Roulette without *En Prison:* Even money bets	2.70%
Craps: Buy bets or Lay bets	5.00%
American Roulette (all bets except Fiveline)	5.26%
American Roulette: Fiveline bet	7.89%
Money Wheel: All bets	11% & up
Craps: Any Seven bet	16.67%
Keno: All bets	22% & up

FIGURE 1
Statistical Casino Advantage

ODDS: WHAT THEY MEAN

Choice is nothing without knowledge.

—United Healthcare of Ohio

In this business, you won't last fifteen minutes if you're not clear on this business of *odds:* what they mean, why they change, and how they are calculated.

Odds represent the probability of an event. When someone says there's a 50% chance of something, it means they don't know. They haven't the foggiest idea. It could go this way, or that. When they predict a 99% chance, that means they're pretty darn sure that their prediction will be right. But people throw out numbers like these all the time, so you have to consider the source whenever you hear someone assigning odds to something.

Casino odds, conversely, are very precise. When they tell you that a bet pays 2–1, they will pay you exactly that amount. But you should understand that every bet in a casino has two sets of odds: the *statistical odds,* and the *payout odds.* The former represents the mathematical chance of a numerical event, and the latter pertains to what the casino is willing to pay to the winner of such a wager. The difference between the two sets of numbers is the house edge, as we have just discussed.

The most common odds found in casinos is 1 to 1, which is also referred to as *even money.* All the major table games have bets within those games that pay 1 to 1 (also denoted as 1–1), including roulette, craps, blackjack, baccarat, and the money wheel.

After 1–1 odds, the most popular are 2–1, 3–2, and 1–2 odds. Any odds where the second number is larger than the first denotes a bet that pays less than 1–1, which is also referred to as *odds-on*. These bets have a better than 50% chance that they will win at any given point in time, but the return is pretty meager.

How are odds calculated? Divide the second number into the first, then multiply the result by the size of your bet. Accordingly, the math for a $10 bet that pays 3–2 would be:

$3 \div 2 = 1\frac{1}{2}$
$1\frac{1}{2} \times \$10 = \$15.$

For a $10 bet that pays 2–1, the math is:

$2 \div 1 = 2$
$2 \times \$10 = \$20.$

And for a $10 bet paying 1–2, it's:

$1 \div 2 = \frac{1}{2}$
$\frac{1}{2} \times \$10 = \$5.$

What about weird amounts like 9–5?

$9 \div 5 = 1.8$
$1.8 \times \$10 = \$18.00.$

Now there is one little sniggle you need to know about: the difference between odds of, say, 4 **to** 1, and 4 **for** 1. In the case of the former, the amount you calculated represents pure profit. That is, you win that amount, *plus* you get your original bet back along with your winnings. For the latter, that represents everything you get back, period. What that means is that 3 **to** 1 is exactly the same payoff as 4 **for** 1. So, buyer beware!

Why do casinos sometimes use **for** instead of **to**? It tends to sound like a better deal, doesn't it?

SUMMARY:
THE POWERS THAT BE

Casinos make good money because gamblers are willing to lose more than they're willing to win.

—President of a Las Vegas strip hotel

The first step toward maintaining command while in a casino is to be wary of the three Cs and the H: *Cocooning, Compulsion, Continuum,* and *House Edge.*

Cocooning: Don't let yourself get too comfortable. Keep in mind why you came: to make money. Try to avoid the distractions, and shun alcoholic beverages while "on duty."

Compulsion: Keep tabs on what you're doing, as if you're watching yourself. When you find that you're straying from the plan, *step away from the tables!* Preferably, *before* making the discovery that all your money is gone!

Continuum is manageable as long as you make it a point to pace yourself, and not stay too long. Don't let the table put you in a trance. Stay on top of things.

House Edge: It doesn't take a genius to figure out that bets having a lower house edge are better deals. As a general rule of thumb, steer clear of the higher-edge bets.

Overall, the best way to avoid these trappings is to make it a habit to keep your sessions brief, and watch yourself like a hawk. You're part of a commando mission, raiding an enemy target. You need to strike quickly, then get on out of there.

The ones who lose are the ones who stay too long.

3

THE FORMIDABLE POWER OF TRENDS

The art of life lies in a constant readjustment to our surr-oundings.

—Kakuzo Okakura

In gaming pursuits, one must make constant readjustments to his environment. The better you can foresee what comes your way, the more prepared you'll be to face it. Knowing what to expect from your opponent (the casino) is what separates the winner from the rest of the herd.

In that spirit, the key to successful gambling lies in the ability to anticipate trend development. You need to size up the table as you play, and chart a course in your mind that represents its logical destination. Then you act upon that projection, for as long as you think you can continue to win.

If you don't get this; if this concept eludes you, there might not be bountiful success at the tables in your immediate future. To win, and continue to win, you have to understand, embrace, and believe in trends. They are your roadmap to the treasure, and your navigation to success.

They'll mislead you at times. But once you understand them, they are more likely to be your friend.

TRENDS IN GAMING

We are confronted with insurmountable opportunities.

—Pogo, from comic strip
by Walt Kelly

Most novice gamblers believe in fighting the trend. For many of them, the conception of that idea is what induced them to try their luck at gambling in the first place. They see an even wagering proposition win four in a row, and figure that a bet on the opposite result is a solid bet. After all, if the even money bet Red won four in a row, the statistical odds against it winning once more are 31–1. Nice to have odds like that on your side! But it needn't stop there. If you should lose, just double your bet with each new loss, and you're sure to catch the winner. After five more losses, the odds will be over 400–1 in your favor!

But that, precisely, is the premise of the gambler's ruin.

Am I saying that trends can routinely buck odds of 400 to 1? Oh yes. Not a problem. Trends don't care about odds. They laugh in the face of statistics. And there's not a force in the world to stop them from doing so.

Of course, you're going to win lots of those 400–1 bets. Lots. But the first one you *do* lose is going to cost you dearly. And when you lose three or four of those betting series the same day, it will shake your faith. In luck, in life, and in the gods themselves. For it will surely feel like you've been picked on by a force well beyond your ability to comprehend.

Now, if you were to try that out just once a day, you might go for months or perhaps even years without losing a wagering series. But most gamblers aren't content to play just one series a day. That won't even put a dent in their travel expenses. So, they keep on pressing their luck, until the overall odds begin accumulating against them. For with each one of those series they win, the odds are slowly and imperceptibly whittling down. This is a cumulative effect that is part of the *Law of Large Numbers.* And you never know when that law will be enforced.

Horseplayers have a saying: *Once you spot the pattern, it's gone.* This is often true for those pursuing speculative ventures, because they miss the big picture. They're seeking trends that are localized and immediate. They miss the larger portrait that's being painted right in front of them.

If you play long enough, one thing you are sure to see with some degree of regularity is what will appear to be historical firsts; things you would not have thought possible had you not seen with your own eyes. In time, you'll become inured to the incredible, and you'll expect the unexpected.

In my early days of gambling, when I believed in fighting the trend like so many others, I sought out something that I called *The Magic Downside Number.* That is, what is the maximum number of decisions an even money proposition can go before the opposite result *has to* appear? My thinking was that, eventually, the Law of Averages would start dictating to the table. But when I played a table at the Tropicana in Las Vegas where Red didn't show up for seventeen spins, I realized my cause was doomed. For the record, Black didn't win all seventeen; a zero got in there. But you know, you can't fight trends like that.

Chances are, the day you pick to *bludgeon your way to a win* is the day a table trend will be so spectacular, it ends up as the lead story in the *New York Times...*

...and you happened to have backed the wrong side.

The Law of Averages has its place in the realm of gaming, but it's no match for the power of trends.

Remember that, next time you want to win.

TRENDS IN EVERYDAY LIFE

It may help you to better understand gaming trends if you are reminded that they are part of everyday living. Most people don't give it a thought, but trends can, in fact, influence the direction of one's personal development.

Ever had days when it seemed like everything went wrong? Or, days when everything went perfectly? These trends are truly remarkable, for they can pervade everything you do and all that you touch for an entire day!

Have you ever tried to buy a certain item, and can't find a store that has it in stock anywhere in the city? Have you ever run an errand at night, and all ten traffic lights you had to pass through were green? Have you ever gone weeks without a date, then have two the same night? Or noticed that both the local basketball teams won their games last night by exactly fourteen points? Or that after listening to the most insidious crap for hours on the radio, suddenly they're playing all your favorite songs?

Perhaps not one of these things has ever happened to you, but you get the drift, don't you?

Why is it important to be aware of the existence of trends in everyday life? Because that awareness can help you avoid being thrown off balance by a statistical fluke that may occur when your money is on the line: *Did you see that? That doggone double zero won four spins in a row!*

So what? Flukes happen. Especially in casinos. You can't let that throw you off your game.

If you pursue gaming as more than just a lark, expect to be floored on a regular basis by trends that defy your imagination, and all manner of explanation!

THE COMPRESSION PRINCIPLE

■□□■□□■□□■□□■□□■□□■□□■□□■□□■□□■□□■□□■□□■□□■□□■□□■□□■□□

FIGURE 2
20 Events, Evenly Spaced

■□■□□■■□■■■□□□□□□□□□□■□□□□□□□□□□□□□■□□□■□■□□■■□■■■□□■□■■□□

FIGURE 3
20 Events, Randomly Spaced

Question of the day: *How can anyone hope to beat the house when the games are slanted in their favor?*

If you study the two figures above long enough, you may find the answer there.

Figure 2 shows 20 numerical events, evenly spaced along a lateral continuum of 60 trials. If casino games were assembly lines, the black squares would represent a one in three chance, meriting a 2–1 return to equitably compensate the risk.

Figure 3 also shows 20 events, but they are randomly spaced throughout the 60 trials. These more closely illustrate what might be authentic table game results.

Take a good look at Figure 3. In the middle of the continuum there are two large gaps. Do you see the impact of those two gaps on the other results? Because of the extended absence of the 2–1 events—which can frequently occur at the tables—the remaining events are compressed into tight groups.

Now, in real life, it's unlikely that Figure 3's dry spell would self-correct (to concur with the probabilities) by the 60th result, but this helps illustrate the *Compression Principle:*

For every absence of a probable event, there is an equivalent compression of subsequent events.

Now, please understand that these are just my words, which I made up after thinking about the matter for about four minutes. . . as opposed to the words of some great historical scholar, like Ben Franklin, or Albert Einstein, in which case much more importance would be ascribed to those words.

But what I'm saying is that what goes up, must come down. Sooner or later, a statistical balance will be impelled.

Three pages back, I was discussing how the even money bet Red hadn't showed up for seventeen spins. Now, do you think Red won the next seventeen? Not likely. But over a period of time, the Law of Averages will ensure that a balance is struck between any two sides, as long as the trials are unbiased. Therefore, the deficit that accrued when Red lost all those bets, represents a shortage that at some point will have to be paid.

The Law of Averages does indeed exist. It cannot and will not be defied forever.

So how does that help a gambler beat the house edge? Like this: when he sees that an event is overdue or overcompensating, it tips the hand of the table. It tells him that something extraordinary is going on, which affords him an opportunity, and an insight: he can *play to the trend* while it's in progress, and, prepare himself for the inevitable trend reversal.

And that can give *him* an edge.

Watch the table. Wait for the signal. Make your play.

POSITIVE AND NEGATIVE TRENDS

In gaming, all table patterns can be classified as belonging to one of the following three groups:

1) *Positive Trends:* Events that occur in groups.
2) *Negative Trends:* Prolonged absences of an event.
3) *Neutral Table Patterns:* Routine event sequences.

A positive trend is the strong presence of a numerical event. Negative trends are the absence of an event. Neutrals are routine table patterns. All of these were just covered, though they had not been named.

Each one could be exploited in a gaming situation. Serious players usually favor *positive* trends, but *negative* trends have their place. *Neutral* table patterns are more difficult to exploit, because they represent what is usually just a brief crossover from a positive to a negative, or vice versa.

Seasoned players usually consider positive trends to be more catchable, because they *favor* the event, while the negative trends oppose it. A positive trend, however, may have run its course by the time its presence is realized. That's why it is so important to anticipate trend development at the tables.

At times it may be advantageous to pursue a negative trend, but only in moderation. For in effect, you are fighting the trend. Positive trends are usually considered more fruitful, because they last longer. But to make the most of them, you must be waiting for their arrival. The trap must be set.

SUMMARY OF TRENDS IN GAMING

We learn only when it is too late that the marvel is the passing moment.

—François Mitterand

For me to suggest that positive and negative trends are both bettable conditions may seem like a contradiction. But this is not so, because they both represent a deviation from the norm. This is when you should take notice, because the sands are shifting, and a new table direction is being defined.

Trends, unbelievably though it may sound, can help you see into the future. Such a vision is far from definite, but frequently solid enough to justify a wager.

Some gaming experts only obliquely acknowledge trends, while others leave it to the individual to decide their importance. But I say that you have little hope for success at the gaming tables until you thoroughly understand them, for they represent the peaks and the valleys of gaming.

Face it: life is a gamble. Whenever you contemplate a career option, decline an invitation, buy a used car, or even drink city tap water, you're just rolling the dice. There is an inescapable measure of risk in everything you do.

As long as you're doing all that gambling, you might as well make it pay. In today's world, your chances for success increase in direct proportion to how well you know the odds, and understand the formidable power of trends.

4

ROULETTE: RULES OF PLAY

You gotta know the rules if you wanna play the game.

—Jamal Wallace, from the movie,
Finding Forrester

The first thing you should know about roulette is that there are two variations of the game, and one of them is clearly superior. There are spinoffs within each type that have modified rules, but there are basically just two types, which are American Roulette, and European Roulette.

The winner in this competition is European Roulette, which has half the house edge of the American counterparts, and, with a certain rule in effect, that (lower) edge can be cut in half yet again. But we are not without hope, for many of the online casinos offer the European version, although the ones with the wagering options imprinted in French may take some getting used to. And, there are some casinos in the U.S. which offer European Roulette, but these usually have very high bet minimums. One exception to this is the Monte Carlo casino in Las Vegas, which offers European Roulette with $10 minimums during non-peak periods.

28

The house advantage for American Roulette is 5.26%; for the European version it is 2.70%, and if the latter has the *En Prison* rule, that edge is reduced to a very respectable 1.35%.

European Roulette with *En Prison* is very popular in Europe with systems players, for its leisurely pace and low edge are very appealing. The American version generally moves faster, which is another drawback that compounds the penalty of the higher edge, for it compels players to react faster, to the benefit of the house. But the American versions are not beyond redemption; I just want to stress the importance of seeking out the European version when circumstances allow.

AMERICAN ROULETTE

All table decisions at American Roulette are reached through the use of a roulette wheel and a white ball that rotates within the periphery of that wheel.

The wheel is precision-crafted to ensure that it is perfectly balanced and therefore not biased toward any of the 38 numbers, which are 1 through 36, plus 0 and 00. There is a compartment that represents each of those 38 numbers. If the rotating ball ultimately lands in the one representing the number 10, for example, then that is the winning number for the spin.

While the wheel is spinning in one direction, the dealer sets the ball in motion in the opposite direction. For several seconds the ball will continue to spin around the rim of the wheel, but as it loses momentum it will gravitate downward, and will probably start bouncing against one or some of the "baffles" (see Figure 4), which were designed to impose yet another level of randomness to the result during the ball's descent.

While the wheel is determining the winner of that spin, the dealer will stack the losing chips that were cleared from the table during the last spin, or he straightens chips for the current spin, in an effort to avoid disputes over which numbers the players meant to cover. As the ball slows down and seeks out its destination, the dealer waves his hand over the layout to indicate *No more bets*. All wagers placed after this signal will be refused.

Figure 4, below, shows the configuration of the wheel that is used for American Roulette:

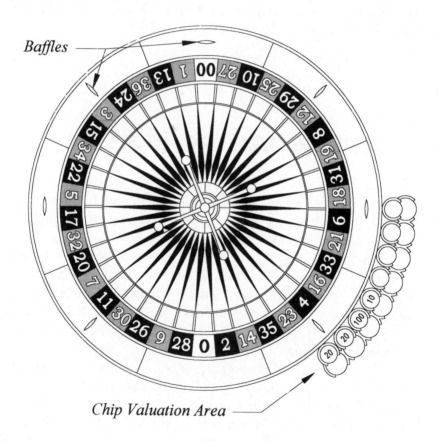

FIGURE 4
The Roulette Wheel
(American Roulette)

Note that the 0 and 00 are at opposite ends of the wheel, and I would like to add that no Red number is adjacent to another Red number. But that applies only to the wheel. On the roulette layout, where bets are placed, the positioning of the Red and Black numbers is more random, as shown in Figure 5, below:

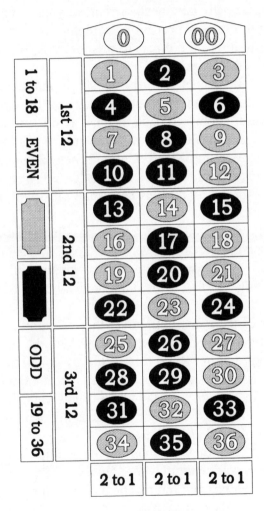

FIGURE 5
The Roulette Layout
(American Roulette)

After the wheel has produced a winning number, the dealer will place a dolly on the corresponding number on the layout, and begin clearing the table of losing chips in preparation for paying any bets that might have won. From the moment the dealer signals *no more bets* to when he removes the dolly from the number that won, you can't place any new bets, or remove your winnings. You must wait until the payoff process is complete, which is official when the dealer removes the dolly. Remember this, if you wish to avoid being scolded by the dealer.

The area of the layout with the 38 single numbers is where the *inside bets* are made; the adjacent sections are for *outside bets.* The table minimum applies to each of these two areas *separately,* which means that at a $10 table (a table where the minimum bet is $10), you can't spread the $10 in minimum bets between the two; you must pick one or the other, or play at least $10 in each. The table minimum and maximum bets are usually denoted on a small placard next to the wheel.

Figure 6 shows the different returns possible from the inside bets. The house edge for all wagers is 5.26%, with one notable exception: the inside bet at the top of the layout called *fiveline* carries a 7.89% edge, giving it the dubious distinction of being the worst bet on the board.

The object of the game is to cover the one number out of 38 choices that will be the winner, dictated by where the ball lands in the wheel. In your attempt to do this, you may cover as few or as many numbers as you wish. That's what's great about casinos: they don't care. They'll let you play all 38 if you want. In doing so, you'll win every single spin, but for a net loss that would equate to the exact amount of the 5.26% house edge.

If you're a recreational gambler and have a hunch that the 17 will come up soon, you could play that number only, every spin, as long as you meet the bet minimum. This is called longshot betting, and that bet will pay 35–1 if it wins.

If you prefer favorite odds, you could spread chips all over the board, or, play the even money *outside bets,* like Red, Black, Even, Odd, Low, or High.

For those who like *odds-on* bets, you could play two 2–1 bets together and get really good coverage, along with a strong chance to win. But the payoff for that 24-number combination is only 1–2 ($1 profit for every $2 wagered).

In between are numerous inside bets that pay 7–2, 5–1, 8–1 and 11–1, to name a few. The 7–2 bet just mentioned, by the way, is not shown in Figure 6, but can be constructed by playing two *corner bets,* which pay 8–1 separately.

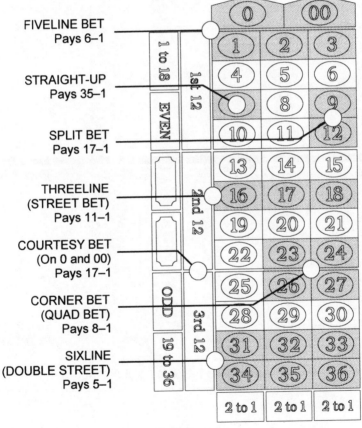

FIGURE 6
Inside Bet Returns
(American Roulette)

Figure 7 shows the positioning and payoffs for *outside bets,* which fall into three categories: *dozens* (1st 12, 2nd 12 and 3rd 12), which pay 2–1; *columns* (denoted by the 2–1 headings at the base of the layout), and the six even money (1–1) bets, which are *red, black, even, odd, low,* and *high.* (The latter two are usually denoted as 1–18 and 19–36 to avoid confusion over exactly where the line is drawn between the two.)

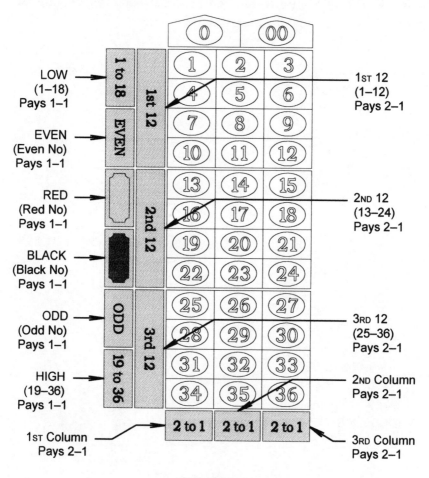

FIGURE 7
Outside Bet Returns
(American Roulette)

Please note that the inside bets shown in Figure 6 are merely examples. They are not fixed positions, except for the *fiveline* bet, which IS a fixed position. All the others can be played anywhere on the board. For example, the *split* bet needn't apply only to over-under numbers as shown in Figure 6; it can also be played with side-by-side numbers. Also, you can play multiple chips on any of the bets, or multiples of the bets themselves, such as three sixlines or five splits. The numerous playing options available at roulette are what help make the game popular.

Regarding the fiveline bet, the reason this one stands out as having the highest house edge is because the amount of numbers covered (five) do not evenly divide into 36. For it to have a house edge consistent with the others, the dealers would have to make part of the payoffs with quarters and dimes. And I must agree with them that this is not practical.

Moving on to *outside* bets, there are six that pay even money and another six that pay 2–1. But the latter are difficult bets to win, and the players seem to be tuned into that. Consequently, the even money bets tend to get more action.

One thing I particularly like about this game is that all of the outside bets have what I call *bet opposites.* With the even money bets, *red* is opposite to *black, even* opposite to *odd,* and *low* (1–18) is opposite to *high* (19–36). With any of the bets, you have exactly eighteen ways to win and twenty ways to lose. The two extra ways to lose are the 0 and 00, which aren't considered red, even, or high, etc. These represent and comprise the house edge, through simple numerical advantage.

But what I like about *bet opposites* is the fact that, if you can disregard or hedge the 0–00, either one side or the other must win. And this helps one follow the philosophy of this book: to *play to the trend.* That is, if one side is hot, you can put your bets there. This is not an option with blackjack. When the dealer's hot, there's nothing you can do but lose, or walk.

As for the 2–1 *bet opposites,* those are formed by playing the other two dozens or columns, as the case may be. However, those bets (when combined into a single bet) pay only 1–2.

As Figure 7 shows, the even money bets are all situated in the outermost column on the long side of the layout. The 2–1 bets are located between them and the heart of the layout (where the inside bets are placed), and, at the bottom of the layout, farthest from the wheel, is where you will find the *column* bets, which cover the twelve numbers in each of the three columns marked 2–1. I believe these are the least popular of all the outside bets. Most players who play the 2–1s seem to prefer the *dozens,* because it's easier to track a group of numbers following in sequence, than a long column of non-consecutive numbers.

That covers the bet types and positions, except for one more that isn't marked, called the *courtesy* bet. For player convenience, casinos allow players to play the 0–00 split on the *courtesy bar:* the line that separates the 2nd 12 from the 3rd 12 (see Figure 6). It may seem odd for an inside bet to be placed amongst the outside bets, but it just happens that only one or two players can physically reach the spot where the 0–00 (hedge) bet is made. This gives them an alternative. There *are* a few hedge bettors out there in the world, who prefer to cover the zeroes as protection against losing a bet to a longshot, especially when betting large.

One more tiny detail: back in Figure 4 (page 30), there was a notation for the *Chip Valuation Area.* That's the name I give it, but I'm not sure of its official name, or even if it has one. That's not important, is it? At any rate, this is where the value of the players' chips is noted for the record. See, roulette tables have special chips that are meant to be played *only* at that table, and their value is determined by the player. This is explained ahead, but I wanted to mention it before we get too far away from the page that has the picture of it. So, for now, please try to be content in knowing that this is a special accounting device that lets the dealer know how much a player's chips are worth when he cashes out, if he has any chips left at that point. . . .

A final note: before choosing a table and making your buy-in, I recommend that you take some time to observe the wagering patterns of the players of this game. If you've never done this, I think you'll find it to be entertaining.

EUROPEAN ROULETTE

Now we come to European Roulette, which by virtue of its single zero, has half the house advantage of American Roulette. And that's big. That means more wins, and less stress.

The configuration of the wheel for European Roulette is as shown in Figure 8:

FIGURE 8
The Roulette Wheel
(European Roulette)

One might think that the roulette wheels for the two versions would be identical except for the zeroes, but this is not the case. The European wheel has a different arrangement, but don't blame Europe for that. They invented the game. It's the Americans that imposed the change. But the layout is the same, except, of course, for the absence of the second zero:

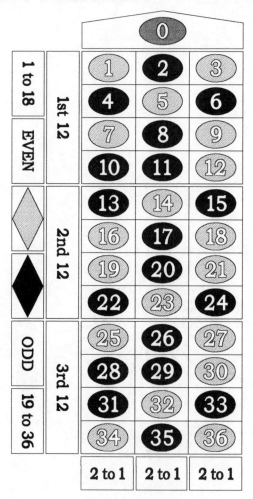

FIGURE 9
The Roulette Layout
(European Roulette)

Now, when I said the layouts are the same, except for zeroes, I was mainly referring to the configuration of the inside numbers, particularly the red and blacks. But what you're seeing in Figure 9 is an Americanized version of European Roulette, which some of the online casinos are kind enough to offer. Normally, the outside bets at European Roulette are arranged a little differently, and are printed in French, as illustrated in Figure 10.

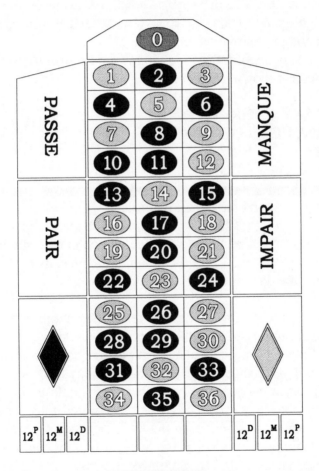

FIGURE 10
The Roulette Layout
(French Roulette)

Well, this is a fine pickle, isn't it? The best roulette version is printed in a foreign language! What's a gambler to do?

First, stay calm. If you become agitated, it can lead to panic. Second, remember that you're in North America (well, *most* of my readers), which doesn't have a lot of European Roulette in the casinos anyway. So we're mostly talking *online* casinos here, and many of them have user-friendly bets. Meaning, when you hover the mouse over the area that says *Manque,* for example, the *1 to 18* area is highlighted. That lets you know what bet you're making without having to know French.

But for the record, the following is the English translation for the outside bets shown in Figure 10:

PASSE = HIGH (19 to 36)
MANQUE = LOW (1 to 18)
PAIR = EVEN
IMPAIR = ODD
BLACK is the dark diamond
RED is the lighter diamond
12^P = 1st 12 (P = Premier, which means First)
12^M = 2nd 12 (M = Milieu, which means Middle)
12^D = 3rd 12 (D = Dernier, which means Last)
(Note: the dozens appear twice in Figure 10.)

And finally, the three empty boxes at the bottom of the layout are for the column bets, as with American Roulette.

For both versions, all outside bet payouts are the same.

Now, if you happen to go to Europe to play roulette, there's a major difference between the two types that should be mentioned. Over there, they don't *typically* use the colored table chips like they do in America, where each player is assigned a certain color, therefore making it impossible for there to be any confusion over who placed that winning bet on number 29. Instead, all players use the same type of chips in the common betting area.

Some European casinos, however, now offer colored chips for roulette, which makes good business sense.

VALUE CHIPS / TABLE CHIPS

In American casinos, there are three types of gaming chips (tokens). The first is metal, and usually intended for slot machine play. The other two are high-impact plastic or a similar material. The first of those are called *value chips* or *generic chips*. These can be used at virtually any table game in the casino, and come in fixed denominations, with the most common being $1, $5, $25 and $100. The larger casinos also have $500 and $1000 chips. Some even go as high as $250,000. Yep. A quarter mil, for one chip!

The other type was designed to be used only for roulette, and are referred to as *house chips, colored chips,* or *table chips.* Not only do they not work at other games; they're not even supposed to leave the table where you got them. These must be exchanged for value chips before leaving the table.

The purpose of the table chips is to help the dealer and the players keep track of who is betting what. See, when you make a buy-in, the dealer will assign a certain color of chips to you, out of eight or so available choices. You can request a color as long as nobody else at that table is already using them. If you don't state a preference, he'll make the choice for you. Then you can play with complete confidence that no one will be able to claim they made that brilliant winning bet you worked so hard to attain.

Value chips may be used at roulette instead of the table chips, provided that no one else at the table was using them first, or, if you're using them for outside bets only.

The above applies to American Roulette. European Roulette characteristically uses the equivalent of value chips.

SUMMARY: RULES OF PLAY

As said earlier, there are spinoffs to each of the two roulette versions. American Roulette has one called Atlantic City roulette, and European Roulette has a rule called *en prison,* which is offered in some casinos and not in others.

Atlantic City Roulette IS American Roulette, with one twist: if a 0 or 00 wins while you're playing even money outside bets, you get half your bet back. This rule was a condition of legalizing gambling in Atlantic City in the late 1970s, and it *does* help soothe the sting of losing a bet to one of the zeroes. This lowers the house edge from 5.26% to 2.63% (for even money bets only).

En prison is the Euro-roulette counterpart: If the 0 wins, the outcome of an even money bet is postponed until the next non-zero number wins, at which moment your wager will either win or lose. This cuts the house edge from 2.70% to 1.35%.

A final note about the odds and payoffs for roulette: On page 33 I described a bet that pays 7–2 when you combine two 8–1 bets. Didn't at least one reader out there think that the 7–2 return (which equals 3½ to 1) sounds like you're being shorted? Don't two 8–1 bets equal one that pays 4–1?

Nope. I can see how it would appear to be so, but when you calculate bet returns, it's safer to use the **for** equation, than the **to** equation (as described back on page 18). In this case, 8 to 1 equals 9 **for** 1. So, for your one chip bet, you get back the original chip plus eight. That makes 9 for 1. But if you lay down an extra chip, you get 9 **for** 2, the equivalent of 7 **to** 2.

Sorry to be difficult, sport, but that's the way the math works. Love it or leave it. . . .

5

THE MECHANICS OF GAMING

Knowledge is the edge.

—Invesco Funds commercial

Now we shall move from the abstract to the precise. Exactly what *are* the moves you will be making as you forage for income in a casino?

THE BUY-IN

Before you can play roulette or any other casino table game, you must first make a *buy-in,* which is the conversion of cash into gaming chips. This was covered briefly in the previous chapter, but it needs to be discussed in more depth.

Your first consideration is to find a table with space to play, and having a desirable table minimum.

At a roulette table, there is a small placard next to the wheel that states the minimum and maximum bets at that particular table. The minimum is usually on the top line, with oversized lettering for clarification.

43

If you have difficulty reading the table minimum inscription because of people in the way, the *color* of the placard is usually a tipoff. Red is the standard color for $5 tables and green is standard for $25, matching the color of the chips. I don't think the colors are standardized for $10 and $15 tables, but it seems to me that most casinos use yellow for $10 and blue for $15.

On that same sign, the *chip minimum* is often noted. This is the minimum valuation that can be ascribed to each of your chips. At a $5 minimum table, the *chip* minimum might be 50¢, which means you'd have to put down at least ten of your chips, each spin, to meet the *bet* minimum. Most casinos I've been to lately have a $1 chip minimum at their $5 and $10 tables, although you can find casinos in Nevada with much lower minimums.

Now, not everyone chooses to play at the minimum bet level. Some might buy in for $300 and request a valuation of $5 per chip. In such a case, he would receive sixty chips, which is how many times $5 divides into $300. Another person might also have bought sixty chips, but did so with a $30 buy-in, which would give *those* chips a valuation of 50¢ apiece.

Every table also has a bet maximum, which is meant to keep players from beating the house with extended betting progressions. In major casinos, the maximum is usually two to five thousand for outside bets, and something like $100 for the inside bets. Why the disparity between the two figures? Well, certain inside bets pay nearly twenty times as much as any outside bets. So, the casinos do that to help avoid those really big surprises, like someone winning a $3000 bet on a straight-up number, for which the house would have to cough up $105,000, and that's way out of line with the $6000 they'd have to pay to the lucky winner of the highest-paying outside bet of the same size.

This does, however, raise a question. Why would the casinos put up restrictions, when in theory, more (or larger) bets translate to more income for the casino?

The play of the larger bettors has to be carefully watched by their most qualified people, and they've only got so many of them to go around. The high rollers play in a special area!

When you have found a suitable table and have decided upon the dollar amount you wish to exchange for chips, lay the money on the felt, outside of the playing area, and wait for the dealer to notice. Don't worry; he'll notice. But to be on the safe side, watch your money carefully until he does. When he picks it up, or looks around to find who put it there, give him your instructions, such as *"Five stacks of chips, please."* A stack is twenty chips, so if you lay down $100—with that request, he should know that you are seeking a total of one hundred $1 chips, which conveniently works out to five stacks. Now these are *table* chips we're talking about, not *value* chips. The latter is the type the dealer would give you for any other table game such as blackjack or craps.

Each player is assigned a different color of chips. Your chips might be blue; the next player might have orange chips; the next one might have brown chips, and all of them might have a different valuation, which is noted in the *chip valuation area* that's shown in Figure 4, back on page 30. The dealer will place a sample chip (of each active color) in separate slots, then place a numbered disc on top of each. The numbers printed on the face of the discs represent the value of one stack, so the dealer will know how much to give each player upon cashout.

It would be a good idea to check what disc the dealer has put on top of your sample chip, because mistakes can be made. There was a time when that happened to me at the Barbary Coast in Las Vegas, and when the dealer tried to cash me out at one-fifth of the amount I was entitled to, I protested rather loudly. The pit boss was there right away, and agreed with me that, yes, my buy-in was what I claimed it to be, and the matter was promptly corrected. That was in my early days of playing, but I have a tendency to be more careful these days.

There is no minimum amount of play required. At times, I've bought in, then cashed out without playing a single spin because of something I noticed at the next table. But the best time to cash out is after the dealer has lifted the dolly from the winning number, for he then has time to address the matter. To do so, push your pile of chips toward the dealer, and say *"Color."*

THE BANKROLL

If you're properly prepared, you won't be easily surprised.

—Seen on a church marquee

Before making your buy-in, you're going to have to figure out where to get the money to do so. That money will come from your *bankroll,* a special fund you set up to be used exclusively for gaming pursuits.

The size of your bankroll depends on how much money you are willing or able to set aside for this purpose. The general rule of thumb is to have a bankroll that is at least ten to twenty times the amount of your average buy-in. With the advent of online betting, however, and if one closely follows the advice of this book, it is possible to work with much less.

How does a bankroll of $300 sound, toward an effort to make several thousand dollars? This is indeed possible for someone who has mastered the 3Q/A strategy ahead in this book, but there are no guarantees in player-side gaming. There is too great a chance for a player to be stymied for long periods of time through nothing more than a bad patch of statistical variance. But the 3Q/A should allow you to do more, with less.

Additionally, online wagering can liberate a player from the need for a large bankroll, since he won't have to deal with crowded tables, high bet minimums, travel expenses, and most importantly, pressure to act quickly.

But if you want to play it safe, then the *ten to twenty times rule* stated above is probably best.

THE SESSION

Now that you've arranged a bankroll, your *session* can begin. This is the gaming activity in which you participate, in between the time you buy in and cash out.

Ideally, your bankroll should be large enough to finance a number of sessions, each of which represents a strategic tug-of-war between you and the casino. Your objective is to win the majority of these battles.

The reason for subdividing your bankroll into sessions is to contain your losses in the event that you get caught up in the heat of the moment, and lose the kind of rigid control over the monetary flow that is a prerequisite to success in this effort. Remember, this loss of control on the part of the players is what paid for all those magnificent chandeliers in the casinos!

How much should you invest in a session? Depends on your betting level, bankroll, and in some cases, intuition. At an online casino with $1 bet minimums, one might be able to accomplish amazing things with just $60. But in a real casino with its higher bet minimums, you'll need a bit more.

Mainly, you want to have enough to dig yourself out of the hole you may fall into right off the bat. Usually, it takes time (and money) to adjust to the proclivity of the table.

How long should a session last? As long as you decide, but you should make that decision *before* buying in, and stick to it no matter what they throw at you.

Later in this book you will find session parameters for all the strategies contained herein. These should provide the answers you need, to these and other questions.

THE SERIES

Success is a journey, not a destination.

—seen on a *Successories* poster

An intrinsic part of each session is something called a *series,* which is really nothing more than a wagering cycle or progression. It consists of a single bet or group of bets whose number should be predetermined by the player.

Not everyone in the gaming business agrees what constitutes a series. Some say it ends only after a win occurs. But as I see it, a series ends when:

1) The last bet of a wagering cycle is reached;
2) A convenient stopping point is reached; or
3) A win occurs.

Some strategies are structured so that a session is comprised of just one series. In that case, the number of sessions you won would coincide with the number of series you won. Other sessions (like those advised for the 3Q/A, ahead) may have an upward limit of two series, while others have no ceiling at all.

It might help to think of a series as being a task of some kind, and the session is the sum of all such tasks from that group. Your first concern is to address the core task (the series), and then go to the next step, which is to complete the session. When the session is complete, it's time to move on.

HEDGE BETS

It does not do to leave a live dragon out of your calculations, if you live near him.

—J.R.R. Tolkien

We interrupt this program to bring you an important message about gaming insurance, otherwise known as *hedge bets:*

Hey, you there: Are you going to let that thousand-dollar bet on Red run the risk of losing to a longshot that could be covered with a very affordable hedge bet? For just $25, I can set you up in a policy that will insure 7/8 of that amount against the possibility that the green monster (called zero) will appear!

Now really, can you afford to pass up a deal like that?

Mind, this only applies for single-zero roulette. At American Roulette, you'll need twice that amount. But it's still a good deal. And now, back to our regularly scheduled program.

As you may have gathered from what you just read, I believe that hedge bets have a legitimate place in gaming. I guess I've lost too many bets to those doggone zeroes.

Hedge bets are like auto insurance. In the event of a disaster (like losing a large bet when a zero wins), you're protected. You're entitled to immediate compensation, which can be a godsend when you've got mondo bucks on the line.

Now, you don't want to play them every time; just when your bets are starting to get large. That way, you have protection when you need it most.

This is just a preview. Ahead in this book, we'll talk at more length about the wagering applications of hedge bets.

THE PARLAY

The parlay is a fairly common wagering ploy, which involves adding the profit from a bet (that just won) to the original wager, forming a new, larger bet.

This is a good way to capitalize on a winning streak of even money bets, such as those found at blackjack, or outside bets (like red or black) at roulette. Doing so gives one the potential to win two units (in the next bet) without risking any more than the single unit of the previous bet.

For bets that pay either more or less than 1–1, however, this technique is not as effective. The 2–1 bets, for example, don't tend to come up in streaks, and the 1–2 bets don't offer the potential to double the size of your win.

If you stick to 1–1 bets, you can, however, expand your potential for gain by adding another stage to your parlay. That is, if your first parlay succeeds, you can parlay everything you won one more time, giving you a chance to win a total of seven units, while technically risking only the original single unit. This is referred to as a multiple-stage parlay, but it's not an easy bet to win. You have to either be lucky, or have a strong indication from the prior table patterns that such an extended streak is likely to occur.

While being a tough bet to win, the profit potential from a multiple-stage parlay can be downright seductive. For example, a three-stage 1–1 parlay will return 15 units; a four-stager will return 31, and a five-stage parlay will return 63 units. Not a bad return from one unit applied to an even money proposition.

But most pros understand that two-stagers are very risky, and anything beyond that is pretty much a fool's game!

PRESS AND PULL

Slow and steady wins the race.

—from *The Tortoise and the Hare*

Press and Pull is conceptually related to the parlay, but it's an ongoing process; a technique that should be considered whenever you're winning with even money bets. In brief, it means *press* up your bet size as you win, then *pull* back at intervals, as a means of locking up your accumulated profit.

One way to do this would be to launch a one-stage parlay every other spin. It's an effective way to maximize your gains, as long as you confine it to when you're already winning. When the wins seem to come easy, you can get more out of the table if you press and pull as you go.

This technique outperforms flat bets during a winning streak, because every other spin you can make twice as much. Of course, a multiple-stage parlay might offer more potential for gain, but you run the risk of losing everything you've built if you don't stop at precisely the right moment.

With press and pull, you strike a balance between low risk and high risk wagering.

Are we clear on this? All we're talking about is betting one unit, and if that wins, parlay the win so that your next bet is two units. If that wins, your next bet is one unit. If you win again, press up to two units. Continue this seesaw process for as long as the wins endure, and hope that when your first loss arrives, it will catch you when you're betting low!

CHARTING A TABLE

If you play enough roulette, you may come across the term *charting a table*. This is an expression used by more experienced players, and it can pertain to one of two things:

1) Analysis of a table, based on data derived from watching the table or from the digital roulette scoresign, or
2) Physical notation of the table decisions, which may take place after the evaluation stage noted above.

In either case, you are attempting to glean information from the table about its active trends, so that its data flowpath can be analyzed and acted upon. Notation, however, can also be useful for an expanded evaluation after the session.

But what's the point of doing this if every table result is an independent event? The future is an unknown at any table, right? True. But most tables tend to *incline* in a certain direction, and that trend can hang on for quite some time.

It comes down to this: you can be oblivious to the table trend, or you can customize your play around it. The former is gambling. The latter is gambling to win.

As you may well imagine, I advocate the latter.

Some players cling to the belief that all tables are equal, and so it makes no difference which table you choose.

A table that shows five zeroes out of the twenty numbers on its digital scoresign is equal to one that shows none?

Would you light a torch to see the sun?

Trends happen. Gamble to *Win*.

THE WAGERING MANDATE

If you have been to a casino, you may have noticed that there is no place to sit except at the tables, the slot machines, or the bar. And if you take any of these seats, you can't stay for long unless you pull some money out of your wallet.

This is the wagering mandate: *Seats are for players.* If you're not gonna play, move along.

The casinos have a legitimate reason for setting up this type of environment: they're in the business of attracting players to their games, so their first obligation is to ensure that seats at a table are not taken by non-players, which might shut out someone who *does* want to play.

Of course, with all the money the casinos make, they could afford to set up lounge areas for the players who are tapped out, or would like to take a break. But that would cut into their valuable floor space, which would otherwise support a row of slot machines or more blackjack tables.

For casinos, making money takes priority over making sure their clientele are comfortable. But that doesn't mean that they are completely insensitive to the needs of their customers. Because of the increased competition these days, they don't want to offend the public that makes their success possible. So, many casinos enforce those rules only during peak periods, when it makes good business sense to do so because of congestion.

This does not mean you can't play sporadic bets. If you don't mind standing, you can play roulette every tenth spin if you desire. And they won't hassle you for that, as long as what you're doing isn't an annoyance to the other players.

THE VALUE CHIP DILEMMA

While roaming the casinos with some casino chips in your pocket, you might happen to spot a table that appears to be ripe for a certain type of bet. You pull a few chips out of your pocket and start placing them on the layout. But before you can get the second chip down, the dealer informs you that you can't use those chips for the spin that's in progress.

Another player, it turns out, is using the same denomination value chips to play inside bets. The dealer can't allow two players to use the same type of chip in the common playing area, lest there be a dispute over whose chip won. He may offer to exchange your value chips for table chips, but this means:

1) There has to be space at the table to set your new chips, because you can't put table chips in your pocket;
2) If you take a seat, you have just inherited the obligation to play every spin; and
3) You may have forfeited the chance to play that particular spin because of the time lost.

Some dealers can handle multiple players using value chips, but that is the exception. Most dealers are trained to regard the issue as being non-negotiable.

And there's another factor that may come into play. Saying this may reveal a superstitious nature on my part, but I don't like interrupting the natural flow of the game immediately after seeing something that tells me the table is ripe for a wager.

At any rate, this is *the value chip dilemma:* you can't always make the bet you want to make.

DEALER MISTAKES, AND DEALER CORRECTIONS

Rule of survival: pack your own parachute.

—T. L. Hakala

The wheel is turning. Your money is on the second sixline, covering 7–12. The ball comes to rest in the slot for number 8. You breathe a sigh of relief. Your gambit paid off.

But then, you don't believe your eyes as the dealer sweeps your chips off the layout, along with all the others that lost. "Hey!" you cry. "You removed my winning chips!"

The dealer realizes his mistake, and the situation is amended. But what if you hadn't been paying attention?

I've encountered dealer mistakes (that's plural) at roulette, mini-baccarat, and craps. Mistakes happen. If you're not paying attention, you could lose a bet that should have won. When that happens, you lose twice: the absence of the payoff for the win, and the loss of your original bet. It may have been just a $25 bet, but the result is a $50 swing in your income for the day.

The scary part is, if you're not careful, you may never realize what you lost, and what could have been.

There was a time at Trump Plaza, however, when the dealer corrected a situation where a player had apparently swiped my $25 chip off the layout, and I protested. I looked at the dealer and the players, but no one said a word. On my next bet, though, the dealer paid me two quarters for my $25 bet on red.

The message here is to keep your eye on your bets. Mistakes, though rare in casinos, do happen.

SUMMARY: THE
MECHANICS OF GAMING

The difference between failure and success often lies in doing a thing nearly right, or doing it exactly right.

—American expression

As tempting as it may be to scour this book for the magical formula that will lead you to your fortune, you would be cheating yourself if you did so. To say that winning in casinos is a tricky business is a huge understatement. If you enter those gates without the proper foundational knowledge, you're going to be eaten alive. You won't have a chance.

On these pages are the parameters for how to win in casinos, but every word on every page holds some significance. You have to approach it in the same way that you would a college education. You need to learn the material, and know it cold.

Don't try to rush your way to success. That's a trap. Just keep thinking, PDPR:

Patience is the vessel.
Discipline is the sea.
Perseverance is the wind, and your
Resolve is the key.

Don't pussyfoot around. Do the job right. Stick to the plan. Adrenalize. Make it happen!

PART II

GAMING TECHNIQUES

6

ANATOMY OF A
TABLE PATTERN

We grow in time to trust the future for our answers.

—Ruth Benedict

In Chapter 1, I tried to convey the point that while gaming tables have no memory, there *is* a force that compels numbers to seek a state of parity with those that have equivalent probabilities. Now, when looked at one decision at a time, I agree: any number can come up. But as the trials accumulate, you will see a decisive inclination toward statistical averaging.

Thus, it is technically incorrect to say that every table result (at an unbiased table) is independent of all others. While there will never be a moment when any number is mandated to win (or not), over time, a mathematical balance will prevail.

What about tables where a wagering proposition wins sixteen in a row? It may look deliberate, but it's nothing more than a fluke. You happened to catch that table in the midst of an abnormal trend. But to a serious player, the origin of a pattern doesn't mean squat. It's what you do with the opportunity.

The ability to *read the table* is one skill that is vital to the long-range success of a player. And the best place to begin that learning process is with even-money table patterns.

THE FIVE PRIMARY EVEN MONEY PATTERNS

Figure 11 shows the *Five Primary Even Money Patterns,* as can be applied to even money wagers for roulette, mini-baccarat, and other table games.

When you see one of the patterns below at a table, it might be beneficial to match it stride for stride. Most patterns are fleeting, but the ones that last can make up for a lot that don't.

Note: R = Red; B = Black (outside bets at roulette)

P1		P2		P3		P4		P5	
R	**B**	**R**	**B**	**R**	**B**	**R**	**B**	**R**	**B**
■		■		■		■		■	
■		■		■			■	■	
■		■		■		■			■
■		■		■			■		■
■		■		■		■		■	
■			■		■		■	■	
■			■	■		■			■
■			■	■			■		■
■			■	■		■		■	
■			■	■			■	■	
■			■	■		■			■

FIGURE 11
The Five Primary Patterns

The Five Primary Patterns from Figure 11 have been assigned the designations P1 through P5. These are the most elementary and easily recognized even money trends.

I recommend that you take a moment to study these patterns, because you may find yourself wishing to "tread water" with small bets to hold your seat at a table, while awaiting a wagering trigger for a certain strategy. Even money bets are just the ticket for doing that, and your session will likely bear more fruit if you're familiar with these arrangements:

P1: This is the most basic pattern, often referred to as a streak. This is simply a prolonged group of duplicate table decisions, and is easy to spot. A P1 pattern must have at least four consecutive decisions, and has no fixed upper limit.

P2: This is very much like the P1, but the streak commences on one side and then switches to the other. As long as both sides each win four or more consecutive decisions, such a trend qualifies as a P2 pattern.

P3: This is another variation of the P1, but it seems to be more common than the P2. With this pattern, one of the two sides has complete domination, except for an occasional hiccup.

P4: Wow! You're gonna see this one a lot! If you visit many casinos that have the digital roulette scoresigns, you can't avoid it. The zigzag pattern of the P4 is so common, the casino people are contemplating building a shrine in its honor.

P5: This is an expanded version of the P4, where the zigzag pattern occurs in pairs instead of single hits. You may find it hard to believe that patterns like this routinely prevail for eight or more table decisions, but it happens.

If you spend time in casinos that have digital scoresigns at the roulette tables, you will eventually see all of these patterns.

PLAYING THE FIVE PRIMARY PATTERNS

If you've ever played mini-baccarat, you can't help but notice that most or perhaps all of the other players are using scorecards to notate the table decisions. Since mini-baccarat only has two basic bets (disregarding the tie bet, which does not cause either to lose), the only way to bet creatively is with pattern play: anticipating the table direction based on previous patterns, and betting accordingly. The scorecards help the players track the patterns.

Roulette has six outside bets that pay even money, which are red/black, even/odd, and high/low. Any of these three groups could be played as one would mini-baccarat, but the higher house edge at roulette (as opposed to mini-baccarat) is something of a deterrent. If you want to hold your place at the table with small bets while waiting for a certain table condition, however, these bets are not a bad choice. In that case, you should have some idea how to play them effectively.

There was a time when I tried to keep on top of all of the even money categories at roulette, thinking it would give me three times the opportunities, but I found myself fighting a war on three fronts! That's a treat I never went looking for again.

Ahead in this book is a chapter on gaming scorecards, and in the back of the book there are scorecard plates that can be copied for the purpose of creating your own sets. I recommend that you make use of these to help you keep track of the table data. They help you see the history of the table decisions at a glance, let you know where you stand monetarily, and provide documentation for future reference.

The following is an evaluation of the five patterns:

P1: It's not easy to specialize in P1s, because most streaks die after five or six consecutive wins—if ever they last that long in the first place. So the problem is that by the time you notice, it may have already peaked.

But for the record, the recommended play for this one is flat bets until the streak dies, or using press and pull.

P2: The P2 has the dubious honor of being less prevalent than perhaps all the others, with the possible exception of the P5. When a P1 streak dies, I usually assume that if the table is likely to continue streaking, a P3 is more likely than a P2. But if it doesn't, you just might encounter a P2.

P3: The P3 is my favorite for parlays. In such a case, I wait for the hiccup (the demise of the P1 streak), then launch a two- or three-stage parlay on the expectation that a P3 will arise from the ashes of the P1. On this basis, a three-stager would net $150 from a $10 bet on an even money proposition.

P4: This is my favorite for flat bets: riding the zigzag streak for as long as it lasts. Sometimes I will interpose a one-stage parlay sporadically in an attempt to maximize my gains.

I find it surprising how few players capitalize on this little gem, because P4s are everywhere!

P5: This is pretty easy to follow. It's actually a variation of an encompassing trend referred to in this book as the *Reoccurring Double,* which is coming up. This one, like the others, is suitable for flat bets and parlays.

If you become familiar with seeing and playing these patterns, chances are, you'll get more out of a table than the next guy who is playing the same types of bets. That is, unless he's having a really, really, super-lucky day. And, betting bigger.

SECONDARY PATTERNS

If only the world was so simple as to have just five patterns to memorize. But as it turns out, there are more, and these might last longer than the primary patterns!

I'll never forget a session in the Flamingo Hilton in Las Vegas where the P8 pattern prevailed for nineteen hands of mini-baccarat. I just copped a ride after the seventh hand and won the next twelve. Of course, I was expecting to lose each new hand along the way, so I didn't get as much out of it as I should have. But that felicitous group of wins wouldn't have been possible had I not been tracking the table results on my scorecard.

P6		**P7**		**P8**		**P9**	
R	**B**	**R**	**B**	**R**	**B**	**R**	**B**
■		■		■		■	
■		■		■		■	
■		■			■	■	
	■		■	■			■
	■		■	■		■	
	■	■			■	■	
■		■		■		■	
■		■			■		■
■			■	■		■	
	■		■	■		■	
	■	■		■		■	

FIGURE 12
Secondary Patterns

ENCOMPASSING TRENDS

Don't wait for your ship to come in. Row out to meet it.

—H. Jackson Browne, Sr.

While you're at the tables trying to figure out if the table trend is evolving into a P3 or a P4, a larger picture is starting to emerge. One that might last for fifty, or even a hundred decisions. It could be a tendency toward choppy table results, or perhaps one of two even money betting choices is maintaining absolute domination. Maybe it's an array of anti-pattern patterns: a series of patterns that bust at the precise moment they appear to be ready to bloom. You'll get all kinds if you play long enough.

The important thing is to keep at least one eye on what I call the Big Picture. What's really going on here? Are we looking at a bunch of flukes that have got to end soon, or is this the equivalent of the amazing golden moment of gaming?

This is the puzzle you should be trying to put together. That is, if your sessions last that long. Some players, like myself, like to keep their sessions brief, as if participating in a raid of some kind. (Remember, the beast could awake at any moment. Grab the jewels and get on out of there!) But even as one who specializes in short sessions, there are times when I find myself locking horns with the tables in a fierce and desperate battle to the death.

When that happens, I need all the help I can get.

There are two encompassing trends in particular that can help you when you find that you need it most: the Reoccurring Single, and the Reoccurring Double.

THE REOCCURRING SINGLE

There is an island of opportunity in the middle of every difficulty.

—from a *Successories* poster

The discovery of the Reoccurring Single came to me one day after I realized that my strategy at a table was, in fact, the path of *most* resistance. I hate it when that happens. But I learned from the experience, so it wasn't a total loss.

The *reoccurring single* is a table condition where one of two sides in an even money proposition wins in single hits, amongst a sea of multiple hits on the other side.

At the time of the aforementioned session, I was playing mini-baccarat at the Palace Station in Las Vegas, where I had been having much success. But I found myself confronted with a pattern that struck me as an opportunity: for the last fifteen hands, the table was favoring the betting option *player,* so that whenever *bank* won, it was only for a single hand before the trend reverted back to *player* for more multiple hits.

This observation was made after *bank* had three single hits. Then *player* won a few more. When bank won the next decision, I followed up with a larger than usual bet on bank. No good. Player won the next two, then it came to bank once again. Convinced that bank was due to score more than one, I followed that bet with an even larger bet on bank. Another bust. When bank reappeared, my next bet on bank wasn't as large. The table was wearing me down. And wouldn't you know, bank lost yet again.

Jee-zooey! Bank had now put out six straight single hits, amid a veritable ocean of player wins.

I was trying to deprogram myself away from the thought of the chase, when bank snared another win, its seventh. Well, I just flat out lost it. I jettisoned my discipline and loaded up on bank. No way could that happen again!

I'm sorry to say, it worked! And bank went on to win five of the next seven hands, which I exploited before cashing out with a small profit. Why was I sorry it worked? As stated in Chapter 2, placing a bet conceived through one's surrender to *compulsion* is a glaring sign of weakness, and an affirmation that you haven't got the right stuff to win in casinos.

—Even when it works!

Losing my discipline, however, was only half the problem. For it later occurred to me that I could have latched onto the player side and garnered a lopsided majority of wins, rather than fight the trend, in an attempt to nail down one big win.

This is what happens when you lose sight of the big picture: What you perceive as an opportunity may in fact be just a drop in the bucket compared to what you could have had!

Figure 13 on the next page is a representation of the scorecard that showed the results of that session. For clarity in conveying this pattern to readers, all *ties* (which do not cause a win or loss to the basic bets) have been removed. And for those not familiar with the game of mini-baccarat, *bank* and *player* are the two basic wagering options. *Player* pays 1–1, as does *bank,* except that *bank* wagers *that win* are subject to a 5% house commission.

The encompassing trend approach to following the pattern is more complex than just matching the pattern line for line. You've got to look at the big picture. During the heart of that run, player won 19 of 25 decisions. It was bad form on my part to overlook something so obvious.

How can one make use of this information? Do the opposite of what I did. Instead of targeting the side that's putting out single hits, expecting the pattern to break, bet on the continuation of that trend, and keep doing that until the wins stop coming.

PLAYER	BANK
■	
■	
	■
	■
■	
■	
	■
■	
■	
■	
	■
■	
■	
■	
	■
■	
■	
	■
■	
■	
	■
■	
■	
	■
■	
■	
	■
■	
■	
■	
■	
■	
	■
	■
	■
■	
	■
	■
	■

FIGURE 13
The Reoccurring Single

THE REOCCURRING DOUBLE

The Reoccurring Double is pretty much what the name says: a reoccurrence of double or multiple hits on one or both sides of an even money proposition. It would be more technically correct to call it the *reoccurring multiple,* I suppose, but that phrase just isn't catchy enough.

Figure 14 shows a classic reoccurring double, which occurred at a session at the Barbary Coast many years ago. The table results commenced with a P4 pattern, then settled into a multiple-hit trend on both sides for eighteen decisions, then put out another brief P4 before resuming the multiple-hit pattern.

This type of pattern is the first cousin to the classic streaking table, which is the converse of a choppy table.

The best way to exploit such a table is to first, seek out a table that appears to be in the early stages of such a trend, then imitate the last table decision with moderate bets. After the table switches to a new side, however, that's when you want to bet larger: directly after the switch. That right there is the key bet, because while you never know how long each group of multiple hits will last, you can count on each side putting out at least two duplicate decisions as long as the trend prevails.

Figure 15 shows another fine example of an *RD*. By wagering on the side that switched for only one bet after the switch, a player would win eight out of nine bets. For comparison, Figure 14 would allow a player to win eight out of ten, *if* that player limited his bets to only after the switch, and commenced playing the RD after the first streak began.

Both the RS and RD can give a player an edge, by enabling him to hit a wagering target with pinpoint accuracy.

PLAYER	BANK
■	
	■
■	
	■
■	
■	
■	
	■
	■
	■
■	
■	
■	
	■
	■
■	
■	
	■
■	
	■
	■
■	
■	
	■
■	
	■
	■
	■
	■
	■
	■
■	
■	
■	
	■
CASH OUT	

FIGURE 14
Reoccurring Double

PLAYER	BANK
SHUFFLE	
	■
	■
■	
■	
	■
	■
■	
■	
	■
	■
■	
■	
	■
■	
■	
■	
	■
	■
	■
	■
	■
	■
	■
	■
■	
■	
■	
	■
CASH OUT	

FIGURE 15
A Classic P5 Pattern

SUMMARY: TABLE PATTERN ANATOMY

You can observe a lot just by watching.

—Berra's Law

The playing style of some of my readers may not require the techniques offered in this chapter, but I feel that this knowledge should be beneficial to anyone who pursues the exploitation of random numerical events.

There are only so many patterns out there. Once you know the basic ones, you will see that every other pattern is a variation of one of those shown here. The more familiar you are with these, the less likely you'll be caught off guard by a table that seems to take delight in dishing out punishment.

Reading the table is a lot like like playing chess. The moves your opponent makes, little by little, gives you more information about his playing style, and intentions. Sooner or later, he starts his attack, and you suddenly see what was behind all those seemingly insignificant moves he was making.

The tables tip their hand, as well. Sometimes a very unusual trend comes up out of nowhere, and you have to perceive it as if its moves are being guided by a higher power.

Who knows? Maybe they are.

But even when you see something that seems so deliberate that you are convinced that there is a definite scheme afoot, please bear in mind the first law of gaming:

There are no sure bets. (This includes bet number ten, from a streak of twenty-two.)

7

TACTICAL DEFENSIVE MANEUVERS

There is no law of science or nature that says you cannot lose a hundred consecutive bets.

—the Author

There is a reason that players tend to lose and the casinos will always win: most players can't handle their losses. They just about go nuts when they lose. Many of them hide it, but after losing, they are filled with explosive rage. They feel an urgent need to retaliate for the hurt they feel inside.

Why? Real simple: the joy of winning does not compensate the pain of losing.

Why? Because losing sends a potent message: at that precise moment, you are a loser. And you want to escape from that bad place as soon as possible, before anyone sees what a loser you are, and before that loss contaminates your psyche. Suddenly, the most urgent thing you have to do is to prove to yourself, and the world, that very soon, you *will* prevail.

Winning is an uplifting experience, but does not provide the commensurate lift to indemnify the pain inflicted by your losses. But there *is* a mechanism to keep us from chasing our losses all the way to financial ruin: Loss limits.

72

SESSION LOSS LIMITS

Experience is a hard teacher, because she gives the test first, and the lesson afterwards.
—from the *Cincinnati Fax News*

This may be hard for you to understand, but there are times when I feel a sense of relief after a loss.

Kidding, right? Nope. When one spends a lot of time playing casino table games, he becomes accustomed to a certain win rate. If he's been blessed with a disproportionate number of wins lately, it begins to feel like a curse. For the longer his win rate continues to defy the odds, the more he dreads the compensating *bad patch* that is sure to follow.

If there is no respite from the wins, it starts to feel like a cloud of doom is following you around. If you don't lose soon, you're going to inherit one hellacious losing streak! Just thinking about it gives you the willies. That is, if you're knowledgeable enough to understand the odds.

To someone who is new to the game, this may sound like a load of crap. Winning is good, period.

But if you play long enough, you'll come to understand that there is a season for everything. A time for winning and a time for losing. If a balance is not struck, all you're doing is building up a stockpile of karma. Sooner or later, all things fall neatly into place. It is the mathematics of statistical destiny.

What about the opposite side, when the losses won't leave you alone? If you keep playing, the wins will come back, but until they do, you're going to need some protection.

This is where your *loss limits* should be enacted, so that when the wins return, you can make the most of it.

So how are loss limits configured? At the beginning of each session, you must set a figure in your head that represents the maximum investment you will make at that table. If that figure is reached, you must find the courage to walk away, and turn your thoughts to other matters until your anger has passed.

What other matters? You came to play. What else is there to do? Well, find something. Anything. Take a walk. Get a snack. Maybe it's time to quit for the day. Just don't make the mistake everybody else makes, and pull more money out of your pocket, like you're feeding a vending machine.

That's how the casinos get your money. All of it. Every last dime. Don't fall into their trap.

Now, there are two philosophies on how loss limits should be structured: some advise quitting when you lose half your buy-in (because it is psychologically bad to bet down to your last chip). Others say that your buy-in is your loss limit. When that's gone, it's time to leave the table. And that means now! Don't even *think* about reaching into your pocket for more money.

Either one is acceptable, if it works for you. I've done it both ways, and ways in between. Most of the time, however, I'm gone if the table is beating me up. I try to be sensitive to which way the winds of fortune are blowing. If I'm having a hard time, I get a clue: time to leave.

So that makes three ways that you can set up your loss limits. Matters not which one you choose, as long as you set up a bail-out procedure that will keep you from gambling all the way to your own oblivion.

You don't think that could happen to you?

Hah hah hah hah hah hah hah!!

What I'm saying, is that if you plan to do much gambling in casinos or online, nothing is more vital to your success than strict adherence to your loss limits. They keep your bankroll from being drained in a foolish and impulsive moment. By limiting your losses at each table, they keep you in the game.

DAILY LOSS LIMITS

Protect the downside, and the upside will take care of itself.

—Donald J. Trump

Apart from your *session loss limits,* there is another level of protection that must also be respected: *daily loss limits.*

Session loss limits can only do so much. If you are having a really bad day, you could be mindful of your session loss limits, and still end up losing a fortune.

The best way to avoid that kind of calamity is to set a figure in your mind that represents the most you'll risk on any given day. Then, stick to that promise.

How much should you put at risk per day? That will depend on your betting level, but a good generalized rule would be to stop for the day after losing five sessions, or more than 50% of all your sessions (after you've accumulated a few).

In saying that, I'm trying to allow for the possibility that some players may play a great many brief sessions, where not that much is being risked. In such case, recommending that you stop after losing five sessions would be bad advice if your overall ratio of wins was, say, eighty percent.

All I'm trying to do is to convey the idea that gambling can get under your skin, and bring out irrational tendencies in all of us. If there are no set boundaries, then two months of hard-fought gains can be wiped out in a matter of hours.

In such a case, the only upside I can see is that the casinos will love you. . .until the *next* pigeon comes along!

WIN GOALS

*We have achieved our position through poise, precision, and
audacity. To this we must add resolve.*

—Ed Harris, from the
1996 movie, *The Rock*

Just a notch below *loss limits,* in terms of importance, lies a
concept known as *win goals.* Now, I realize that many readers may
balk at this idea, but the fact that you're winning (for the moment)
is not a valid reason to stay at a table.

True, when you're doing well, you might be able to get more
out of a table if you stay, but over the long term you're going to be
hurting yourself if you press your luck.

Win goals are much like loss limits, in that you want to set a
figure in your head that represents a reasonable and attainable goal.
If that figure is reached, it's time to move on.

This may sound like a recipe for underachieving, but years of
experience have taught me that it's best to keep your sessions short
and sweet. If you stay too long, you run the risk of getting pulled in
to the virulent effects of continuum. Complacency starts to set in.
Before you know it, you're desperately trying to compensate for a
string of losses that followed all those wins.

If that happens, you're cooked.

Remember, that thing called the house edge never sleeps. The
more you play, the more it insinuates itself into your table results.
But if you keep yourself a moving target, you stand a better chance
of staying one step ahead of the beast.

And that's the better place.

SETTLE FOR 90

If the enemy is in range, so are you.

—Anonymous

The concept of *Settle for 90* was introduced in my first book, *Gamble to Win*. It is offered here once again, because I think it is important enough to bear repeating.

Settle for 90 is the underachiever's version of a win goal, but it just might save your butt on many occasions.

In an extended series of trials (sessions), there will be times when you are just a notch below your win goal, but you suddenly encounter resistance from the table. You're not losing, but you're not making progress, either. You win, the table wins, then you win, and so on. It could go on like that forever, or the table might make a vicious move against you.

In cases like that, best thing to do is to *settle for 90*. That is: when you're near to your win goal, don't go out on a limb trying to get that last ten percent. Cash out, and be content in the knowledge that you pulled off another win.

Don't push it. Tables don't like to be pushed. The table has conceded victory. Are you going to kill it twice? If so, the gods of gaming might decide that it's time to teach you a lesson.

They charge when wounded, you know. No, wait. That's a hippo, or a rhino, or something.

Point is, walk softly amongst the slumbering beasts. Don't arouse their ire. You never know what they're capable of, once you start picking on them.

Settle for 90.

THE REALITY CHECK

It is unwise to be too sure of one's wisdom. It is healthy to be reminded that the strongest might weaken and the wisest might err.

—Mohandas Gandhi

As much importance as I ascribe to the concepts of loss limits and win goals, they might not be necessary if one can assimilate the *reality check* into his playing style. But I sincerely doubt that many players could do that every single session. Nevertheless, it's something one should know about.

The reality check is another promise you make to yourself, but it is all-encompassing. It is a vow to watch yourself like a hawk with every bet you make.

Picture that you're able to step outside of yourself, and watch everything you're doing. What is that fool doing with *your money?* Is he investing it wisely, or has he become caught in a snare, and is losing control? Is he adhering to the procedure, in spite of the ugly misfortune that has touched him? Is he accomplishing what he set out to do? *Is he winning?*

Four times a minute is a hard, but serious, figure. That's how often you need to picture yourself as another player at the tables would see you, and question the wisdom of the moves he makes. You must challenge every bet he puts down, and every decision he contemplates.

Even if you manage to obey your loss limits and win goals *scrupulously,* the reality check is a great backup. It keeps you on top of things.

It might help tune you into this notion if I tell you how the thought came to me. Some years ago, while playing mini-baccarat in Atlantic City, I was doing quite well. But then I noticed I had an audience. A woman in her twenties was standing next to my seat, and when I glanced up she asked me some questions about the game. She said it looked like fun.

She wanted to play, but the table was full, so I offered to add her chips to my bet stacks, slightly off center.

But as I played, I advised her of the sureness of each bet as the table results accrued. At times, I would tell her it looked like a solid bet, and she would hand me a chip. Other times, I expressed doubt about the outcome, and she held back.

She had only two or three reds in her hand when we started, but after twenty or thirty minutes she had fifteen. About then, I had surpassed my win goal, and cashed out. I invited her to check out some other casinos with me. That's when she told me that her bus would be leaving soon.

She was just killing time. . .

. . .and trying to get back some of her slot machine losses, with as little risk as possible.

In spite of my disappointment that things did not work out better for me, the encounter helped me see the value of a detached stance while at the tables. If you think in terms of helping a pretty girl make money, it's easier to gain the objectivity to make good things happen. I realized then that it was easier for me to help *her* than to help myself. With my guidance, she quintupled her buy-in in less time than it took for me to double mine.

Setting up your own reality check means reminding yourself before walking up to the tables that you're going to take time out, every few seconds, to evaluate your progress.

Think of yourself as the instructor, watching his student test his skill at the tables. What does your instinct tell you? Is the table running the way it should, for him to win?

Choose wisely. If you don't guide him to the best choices, he's not going to have much respect for you.

That mentality is the best defense there is.

SUMMARY OF TACTICAL DEFENSIVE MANEUVERS

It is often difficult to overcome the inertia to stay in one place.

—Ian Anderson, from
Turning the Tables on Las Vegas

To be a real player in this business, you have to stay on top of what's going on around you, all the time. You have to ask yourself: *am I winning at this table?* If the answer is no, you have to find the strength to lift your butt off the seat and move on.

Even after spending years on the player side of the tables, any veteran of the games knows that he'll never have seen it all. Around every corner in time lurks a new surprise, waiting to stun you with an unexpected twist.

Your best defense is to remain humble. Acknowledge that the element of surprise is on the side of the other guy. Expect the worst result at the worst possible moment.

If you think in those terms, there may be hope.

Have a plan, and follow through on it. Don't let yourself be distracted from the task at hand. Stay in control.

Most important: watch yourself. Be ready for the beginnings of your own self-destruction at any moment, and bail out before the plane goes down.

You're a survivor. Whatever the tables throw at you, you'll get through it. But it will take all the resolve you can muster.

Be prepared for the challenge of a lifetime, each and every time you set foot in a casino.

8

A WORD ABOUT
GAMING SYSTEMS

There is no honest "system" that will consistently overcome casino odds.

—Lyle Stuart

This book would not be complete if it didn't have something to say about *systems,* which are controlled gaming procedures that aspire to outperform random wagering.

Lyle Stuart's quote above reflects my feelings on the subject of gaming systems: they don't work. While I agree that structure is important in your game plan, too much of it introduces an excess of rigidity. It's only a matter of time before a table zeroes in on the weak link, and hammers it into the shape of a frisbee.

If progressing blindly through a mechanical process worked (at the tables), it would have been a huge media event. It would have changed the face of gaming as we know it. Every sharpie in the world would be ravaging the casinos until they either changed the games, or closed their doors.

Until you read about that on the front page of the *NY Times,* assume that systems still do not work, just as effectively as they haven't been working for all these years!

THE MARTINGALE

The Martingale is usually the first choice of novice gamblers. It sounds perfect: wait until a table game result is statistically due, then launch a wagering series. If you lose, double your bet. Lose again, keep doubling. Given time, the odds will be so heavily in your favor that you'll *have* to win.

Hold on. Not so fast. Do you recall the table I told you about (on page 22) where an even money proposition didn't show up for seventeen spins? Do you know how much it would cost to finance a series of *eighteen* bets that double each time?

Assuming that you start at the $5 level, your eighteenth bet (which would net a $5 profit) would cost you $655,360. Financing those bets would cost over a million bucks! But it's a moot point, because you would never get a waiver against the house maximum in the midst of all that. And that point would be reached about halfway through the series.

I think the casinos do that to prevent fools from being parted from their money on such a grand scale.

The reality is, that if you play long enough, you're going to hit the mother of all bad tables.

Of course, you could limit your series to, say, five stages, and you would win most of your sessions. But speaking as one who has performed countless thousands of numerical trials, I've found that on average, no matter how many stages you use, you'll encounter a full series loss at roughly the same rate it takes to earn the units to pay for it. And when you figure in the house edge, the two sets of figures match up almost perfectly!

Amazing stuff, huh?

THE MINI-MARTINGALE

This is a Martingale that is limited to three stages. At the $5 level, a series of even money bets is $5–$10–$20. If you don't win by the third stage, you must write off the series as a loss.

A series costs $35. You have only three chances to win, and it will take seven wins to compensate one series loss.

At a choppy table, a mini-Martingale could keep you winning indefinitely. But when the table patterns change, you're gonna get a load of buckshot in your butt.

While this ain't the ticket to long-range success, you could do worse. It's like running a yellow light. If you don't do it too often, you might be able to dodge the man for some time.

THE ANTI-MARTINGALE

This one is the opposite of the Martingale: you double your bet after a *win,* instead of a *loss*.

This is just a multiple stage parlay. It offers the chance to win $640 from a $5 bet (for example), *if* you can anticipate a streak of seven straight wins, and bet accordingly.

There is no limit as to how many stages to use, but the more you use, the more you compound the risk. So, the key question is: at what point do you stop and take your profit?

If you're a better guesser than the best psychic in the world, maybe, just maybe, you can make this one work!

THE 31 SYSTEM

This is one you should know about, because it sounds rather interesting, allowing you to lose eight straight decisions and still have a shot at winning the series. The only catch is that you have to end up with back-to-back wins.

Figure 16 shows the structure of the 31 system, as applied to even money bets. You start at 1 unit (Level 1), and if you lose, go to the next number to the right, which is also a 1. As you lose, keep moving to the right, then down to the next line. Once you get past the second bet, if and when your first win comes, you have to parlay that win and hope for another (back-to-back) win. If that succeeds, start another series.

LEVEL 1:	1	1	1
LEVEL 2:	2	2
LEVEL 3:	4	4
LEVEL 4:	8	8

FIGURE 16
The 31 System Levels

At the $5 level, a full series costs $155. Now, catching a win at the earlier stages of each new level will net a larger gain than at a later stage, but as long as you win the series, you'll show a profit regardless where the win occurred.

It's an ingenious system, but a few trials on paper against live gaming results will expose the fact that it really doesn't work. The eight losses it allows is generous, but consecutive wins at the end are too much to routinely ask from the tables.

THE D'ALEMBERT

The D'Alembert is also known as the Pyramid, because of the shape of its fluctuating wagering structure. It's pretty simple: increase your bet one unit after every loss, and decrease one unit after every win.

This is one of those pummel-your-way-to-victory deals, and it frequently *does* work. But there will be times when your bets have been pushed to the ionosphere, and there will be no one on hand to talk you down. Because, by that time, a lot of your money will be gone, so who would want to?

This is one of the chilling facts of gaming: in the same spirit that everyone loves a winner, nobody likes a loser!

THE CONTRA D'ALEMBERT

This is another "system opposite" (like the Anti-Martingale), but it applies to the D'Alembert. With this one, you increase after every *win,* and decrease after every *loss.*

Because it offers reasonable protection of the downside, it is one of the better ones to try (if you're determined to play systems), because when the losses come, your bets regress to the base level, where they will stay until the wins return.

It's not a bad way to exploit a winning run, if it is used as a sporadic technique. In fact, I have been known to employ betting schemes that are based around this concept!

THE 1-2-3-4 SYSTEM

I can't let you out of this chapter without telling you about a wagering device that is frequently used by seasoned players. Think of this one as a one-way D'Alembert, which has been blessed with a four-unit ceiling.

This system calls for you to increase your bet size by one unit after every loss until you win, or reach the four-unit level. If you don't get a win there, the series is over.

The word "system" is used rather loosely here, because this is more a technique than a system. If played on that basis, I have no strong objections to it. It gives you a strong chance to win, without compelling you to mop up a huge mess when it fails (unless you can't stomach a ten-unit loss). Now, once you reach the third stage, all you're shooting for is to get all or most of your money back, with no hope of showing a profit for the series. But it usually keeps you in the game, and that counts for something.

Although it was designed for even money bets, the 1–2–3–4 can be used for other bets, preferably those which pay somewhere between even money and 2–1. Depending on the payoffs of the bet you're pursuing, it would be possible to garner a profit regardless the stage you're at when the win occurs.

Years ago, I used this technique quite a bit. But these days, I find that I'm more conservative. I seldom chase anything for more than two or three stages, even with bets that pay 2–1. Time and seasoning have taught me that if you don't catch something early, the prudent move is to abandon the chase. At the next opportunity, you'll get your man.

It helps to have that inner knowledge.

OSCAR'S GRIND

This is the most conservative (but perhaps the most viable) even money system shown in this book. Because it lacks ambition, it may be the most ambitious strategy of them all.

All you're shooting for is a one-unit gain per series. Not very exciting, but impressive nevertheless in its appetence for thrift. It is the J.C. Penney of gaming systems, because you risk only the bare minimum required to show a tiny profit. That keeps your expenses whittled to the bone, and in doing so, helps to shield you from the wrath of the raging downside.

The rules are as follows:

1) Increase your bet size by one unit after a win, provided that it won't result in a series gain that exceeds one unit.
2) Never change your bet size after a loss.

That's all you need to remember. Follow those two rules and you can't miss.

Although I give this system high marks, it is far from perfect. If you catch a table that's dishing out solitary wins surrounded by multiple losses, you're gonna get battered and bruised. In that case, the system keeps pushing your bets to higher levels, where you get ambushed each time. Not a pleasant thought, but that situation is not very common. For most other scenarios, this system performs admirably, or passable at worst.

If you do try this one, be sure to establish strict loss limits beforehand. What you really do not need is a moment of strategic indecision just as your bets are getting huge!

SUMMARY OF GAMING SYSTEMS

People think: "We're going to follow this plan step-by-step, and it's a done deal." But it's been said that no battle plan survives contact with the enemy.

—Morgan Freeman

No matter what table game strategy you choose, it's only a matter of time before the casino recalibrates its defenses and starts a vicious counterattack. It reminds me of those Star Trek episodes where they're fighting the Borg. The good guys can kill the first one, but after that the collective adjusts to their phasor frequency and renders their weapons impotent. I think those (Borg) episodes were written after the lead writer of the series returned from a rough weekend in Vegas.

Nowhere is it harder to maintain an edge than when you try to outsmart the casino with system play. True, every table pattern is different, but given time, any table will shake off your attack with alarming ease. It is an inevitability.

The best way to beat the table is to think of it as a person, who will not respond to being treated like a machine. It has its own identity, and it wants you to appreciate how special it is. So you have to take time and get to know it. Learn its moves. Put yourself in its place. BE the table.

If you succeed in becoming one with the table, you'll start to see what it wants and where it's going. Try a few dry bets, where you predict what it will do next. When your guesses are on target, it might be time to put down some money!

PART III

STRATEGIES

9

GAMING PROCEDURES

You should only pick fights you're sure you're going to win.

—from TV miniseries *Central Park West*

Now that we have covered systems, we are free to move to a higher plane. In this book, gaming *procedures* are considered to be superior to gaming *systems,* because they enable the player to be more sensitive to the permutations of the table. While most experts agree that structure is important in one's approach to winning, too much of it gives you no room to maneuver.

Procedures, unlike systems, offer the player the agility that comes from an abbreviated lifecycle. They allow him to react quickly to the changing battlefield conditions, and give him the *out* that is needed from time to time. They can be micro-managed, which is helpful when one's routine involves making numerous spontaneous decisions.

Systems fail because they cannot adjust to the late-breaking information. They are blind to the fact that every table has its own signature. To get the most from your gaming pursuits, you have to tune in to the table frequency, and play accordingly.

SIZING UP THE TABLE

Starting out on the right foot is always the best approach in any endeavor. You wouldn't want to discover that there's no water in the pool after diving in, would you? Nor would you purchase a house, sight unseen. Information that is gathered beforehand helps guide us to the wisest choices.

Many people who agree with the above, however, would balk at the idea of charting a table before placing bets. What's the point, when table results are not influenced by past events?

The answer to that question can be found in the difference between viewing table decisions one at a time, or in groups. On a one-by-one basis, I agree that any number could come up on the next decision. But close scrutiny of any *group* of roulette numbers will usually reveal a distinct pattern that sets that table apart from the others. By catering your play to the existing trend, you have a chance to capitalize on known information. And that's a massive improvement over betting blind.

At some tables, a certain 2–1 bet I play will win on the first bet of a triggered series again, again and again. At another table, using the same wagering trigger, I will lose fourteen bets in a row. There doesn't seem to be a logical reason for this, but since it happens, why not use the information to your advantage? Would it not seem foolish to try picking apples off a dead tree, when there's another one nearby, loaded with fruit?

Pursuing the established trend is how a seasoned player gets the edge he needs to sustain a winning percentage. Without that, he would have to rely solely on luck.

Luck helps, but it takes more than that to win.

THE ANGEL AND THE SLEDGEHAMMER

The following is a description of a pair of roulette bets that are referred to in this book as the Angel and the Sledgehammer. They are presented as a package, rather than separately, because each is the 'bet opposite' to the other.

THE SLEDGEHAMMER

Back in the early 1990s, the Frontier Casino (now called the New Frontier) was very, very good to me, as the great athlete, Elio Spaghetti*, used to say of baseball. Adjacent to the gaming area was an in-house restaurant called Michelle's Café, which offered a $3.95 prime rib dinner special. The only catch was the typical forty-minute wait until they called your number and seated you. Well now, what are you going to do while waiting, when there's a rollicking casino right there?

That's right: you play, and lose. Play, and lose. But not me. Back then I did nothing but win in that casino, and since it was a short walk from where I lived, this worked out well. As I waited for my number to be called for the café special, I'd earn $100 a night playing low-stakes craps or roulette, while taking advantage of their free-drink policy. Life was good.

*(Not his real name)

On one such occasion, I was playing a roulette bet called the Sledgehammer, a $20 bet comprised of a $5 chip on each of the four middle sixlines (covering numbers 7 through 30). That night, I had chosen to play roulette so I could take the empty seat next to the blonde hottie in the middle seat. While playing, I was admiring the success rate of her inside bets. She said she was from Canada, and to this day I still wonder if Canadians have a special knack for roulette. After seeing her rack up a few more wins, I complimented her on her playing style. Then she turned to me and remarked that she hadn't seen me lose since I sat down. I shrugged it off, saying that it was a wide coverage bet that produced a meager return. But then I looked at my pile of chips and realized I had accumulated quite a haul. Time to bail out, since anyway, Little-Missy-from-Canada was married.

At cashout, some quick math told me that I'd just completed a run of twenty-two consecutive wins!

Such is the power of the Sledgehammer at the right table. But don't be fooled. Although I still play it at times, I think of it as a fill-in bet. It deserves mention, though, because of what evolved from its creation.

More on that in a minute.

The Sledgehammer derives its name from the sheer weight of its massive coverage. The unhedged version covers 24 numbers, but with a hedge on the 0–00 split, it covers 26 of the 38 numbers at American roulette, which is more than two-thirds of the layout. Its upside is that at any point in time, a Sledge bet is more likely to win than lose. The downside is that the losses are tough to handle: it takes roughly two wins to compensate a loss.

So, why am I leading you down a dark alley, toward a bet you may never play? Well, knowing about it can be helpful at times, and some readers—who like the nurturing effects of a bet that wins often—may decide to make it the central bet of their wagering strategy. As illustrated in the story you just read, it can be used to milk a table (for some time) with very little effort. But when the losses start coming, you've got to be ready to move out the platoon on a moment's notice.

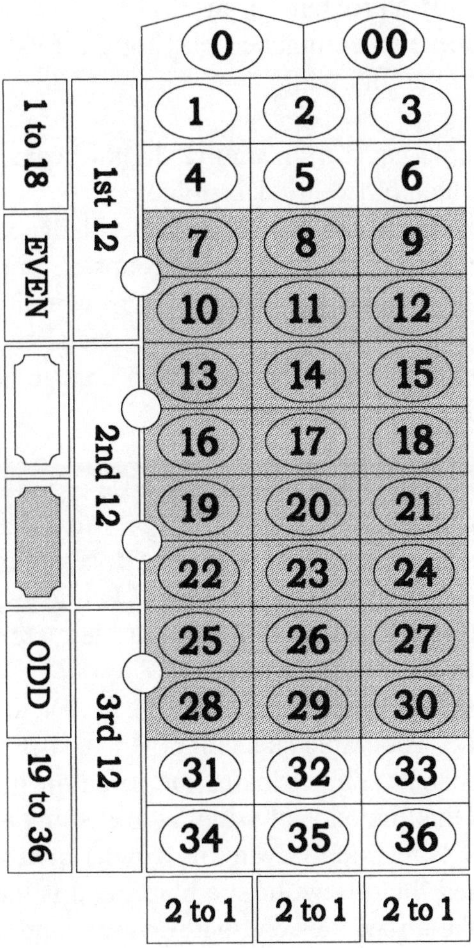

FIGURE 17
The Sledgehammer

If you play the Sledge, it's best that you don't press your luck as I unwittingly did in the story. That was a case of inheriting a lucky win from inattention. With no losses to address, it was easy to be distracted. The general rule of thumb, though, is to hold back after getting two consecutive wins out of a table. Nailing down that third win is usually a problem for me.

The best time to commence playing the Sledge is at a table that conforms to the following:

1) The table has a scoresign (a digital board that shows the last fifteen or twenty decisions).
2) On that sign, you can see that the Sledge numbers (7–30) are (generally) coming up in groups of four or more.
3) An Angel number (1–6 and 31–36) won three spins back.
4) Sledge numbers won the last two decisions, and
5) A 0 or 00 has not won more than once in all the decisions showing on the scoresign.

When you find a table that meets those criteria, you've found the ideal wagering situation for the Sledge. Most times, you should be able to squeeze out a pair of wins. But don't whine to me if you go through all that and your very first bet loses. That doesn't happen often (under those conditions), but there are no sure bets in the world of player-side gaming.

Now, there are other wagering triggers for this bet, which I have used with considerable success. One is to bet blind. Omigod! Did I really say that? Yup. It pains me to admit it, but at times I trust in the fact that the odds of winning are on my side, and take a shot at a table where I don't even know what number was the last to win. It's called 'betting without a plan', and is indistinguishable from 'betting like a fool', except that for some quirk of a reason, it usually seems to work!

(But in doing that, I rely somewhat on instinct.)

Figure 17 shows the basic unhedged Sledgehammer. Coming up, you will learn more about the interplay of this bet with the associated wagering options.

THE ANGEL

The Angel was originally created from the leftovers of the Sledge. It was born from the necessity to find an effective response to losing that bet.

After doing a study of Sledge losses (to ascertain how best to deal with them), it came to my attention that non-Sledge numbers frequently came up back-to-back. How wonderful! Those twelve numbers (collectively) paid 2–1, which meant that this two-chip bet (covering two sixlines) would compensate every dollar of a four-chip loss from a Sledge!

A new bet was born. Since it had saved my butt a few times, it was named the Angel. And though it was created as a bailout for the Sledge, it ultimately graduated to a higher place.

And now, the obvious question: why do I bother with these messy inside bets when a reasonable equivalent could be fashioned from outside bets, with less hassle? Well, isn't it obvious? Angel numbers are magic. They're special. They behave differently from the others because they've been aged in fine old kegs, while the others were pulled straight out of the box.

And that's not all. (I'm serious this time.) The dozens have no equivalent for the Sledgehammer *hot zones,* which can help you cobble together a sensational winning run (more on this real soon). Also, if you want to hedge an outside bet, your hedge (which is considered an inside bet) has to meet the table minimum by itself. However, when your wager is an inside bet to begin with, adding a hedge is just a matter of tacking on a tiny bet.

Figure 18 shows the configuration of the Angel bet (which covers all the numbers omitted by the Sledge).

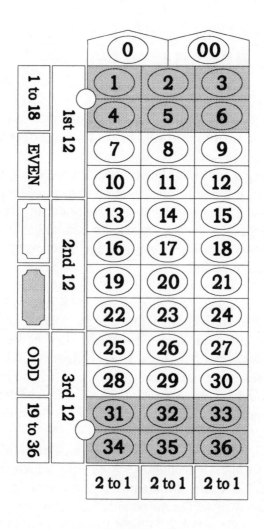

FIGURE 18
The Angel

THE SLEDGE "B"

As an alternative to the Angel, since (like any other gaming option) that bet doesn't always work, the Sledge "B" was created. The unhedged version also covers 24 numbers: 1 through 12 and 25 through 36. It is recommended that you use (four) sixline bets to cover this area (rather than play the 1st and 3rd 12 outside bets), so as to keep your hedging options (on the 0–00 split) open, among other things. Figure 19 shows the Sledge "B".

The Sledge "B" was designed as a complement to the basic Sledge, so that you could switch from one to the other when losing, on an ongoing basis. But there is a way to play where you might be able to dodge the grim reaper by taking your cue from the table, and switching *before* a loss. This can be accomplished by utilizing the *hot zones,* as I call them. These are the areas of the layout where the two Sledgehammer versions overlap: the 7–12 and 25–30 sixlines. Figures 20 and 21 show these zones.

TANDEM SLEDGE PLAY

When playing the Sledges, I prefer to start out with the basic Sledge, as illustrated on page 95. If you lose to an Angel number, move your subsequent bets to the Sledge B. If you don't lose, keep playing the Sledge until the numbers start coming up in the hot zones. That tells you that the pattern is moving to the extremities of the layout, which cues you to switch to the B version.

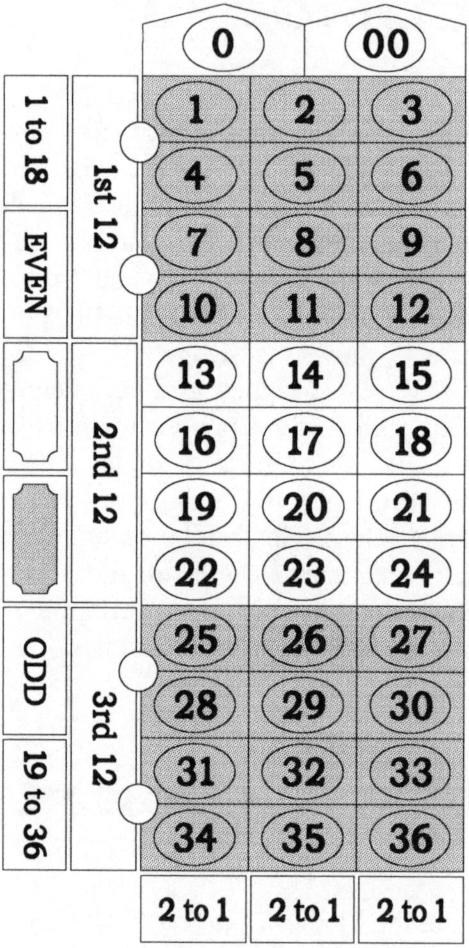

FIGURE 19
The Sledgehammer B

Ideally, the table decisions will subsequently move into the Angel section, then back into the hot zones, which is your signal to return to the basic Sledge.

Now you've heard everything! The author expects you to believe that roulette numbers are obedient little buggers that go where they're told? Well, some tables are more cooperative than others, but you might be surprised at what's possible when you're dealing with such wide coverage. With all those numbers in play, there will be times when it doesn't matter which Sledge version you pick for seven or eight decisions, because the wins are landing in the hot zones, which are covered by both bets!

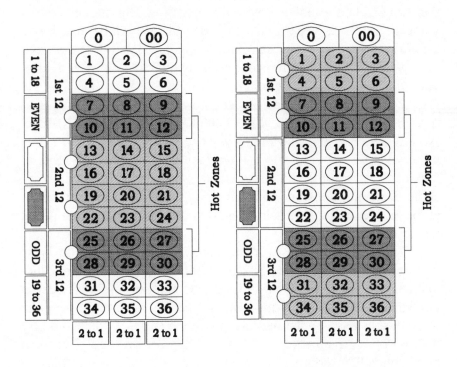

FIGURE 20	FIGURE 21
Sledge A Hot Zones	*Sledge B Hot Zones*

The key advantage of *tandem Sledge play* is that only a small portion of the layout is uncovered, and that section is a moving target. In theory, a player could win fifty or more consecutive decisions in this way, without asking anything more from the table than a continuation of routine table patterns!

That scenario assumes that the zeroes are hedged throughout the duration of play, and that a loss to a zero is treated as a push, since it would roughly equate to that.

How big should your bets be? Big enough so you can retire in the next two or three weeks, I would say. Big enough so you can buy that big house on the hill, stocked with an inexhaustible supply of whatever you'd like an inexhaustible supply of. Big enough so that you can end a sentence with a preposition. Big enough so that you can pay for a week's visit to Space Station Alpha, *and* buy a tropical island where you can build a gigantic laboratory for your time-warping global mind control machine, to help you realize your long-sought goal of world domination.

Oh, you want the specific bet amounts?

It's a four-unit bet, which I think of as having a $20 base. After a winning run, you might want to try to squeeze out a few more wins by regressing to a lower bet level, like $4, $8, $12 or $16, depending somewhat on the table minimum. (We'll talk more about bet regressions later on.) Hedging the 0–00 is recommended at the $20 level, but not below, as it would eat up too much of the already meager profit.

Some players may want to specialize in playing the basic Sledge only, foregoing the Sledge B and Angel, by utilizing fluctuations in the bet amounts. In time, one can become proficient at knowing when to press up a Sledge bet to maximize the gain, through sensitivity to the inclinations of the table. If you should try that, however, tread softly. If you play this bet recklessly, you can bury yourself in about four minutes flat. Actually, some players I've known can do it in half that time!

But this is not a good thing, because contrary to the popular notion, this does not defray your funeral expenses. When *that* time comes, you'll need a different kind of burial!

SLEDGE PLAY: WHEN TO STOP

The most important thing to know about this betting scheme is *when to stop*. Whenever playing a Sledge bet, every single loss must be scrutinized, especially if you weren't expecting it. When a loss occurs, do a spontaneous review of what happened, and then make a recommendation of appropriate follow-up action. In many cases, you may decide that you are content with the winning run you have already accumulated, so it is time to pack it in at that table. Other times you might think you can squeeze more out of the table, but if so, you must establish a firm loss limit (of one or two more losses, for example), and stick to that decision.

If you reach a point where a loss surprises you, or leaves you confused as to what to do next, don't hesitate to bail. When playing such a costly bet, you have to maintain a low tolerance for losses. If the table puts up a fight, it's time to quit. You're not looking for a fight. You're looking for submissive prey.

A conservative yet effective way to play is to settle for a few scores and then leave before your first loss. This may prevent you from racking up one of those monster winning streaks, but it's a good long-range approach.

The Sledgehammer family of bets has helped me a great deal. It would be unwise to rely too heavily on them as bailout bets, but they have served that purpose for me on many occasions. Recently, for example, I was playing online, and had gotten into a large hole. In a departure from what I should have done, I played five Sledges over the next ten spins, which saved the session. Sometimes you gotta fly by the seat of your pants.

THE 3Q BET

The 3Q bet is so named because it is composed of three *Quad* bets (or *corner* bets, as they are sometimes called). This group of bets covers the numbers shown in Figure 22. When played as a set, they yield a 2–1 return.

This particular group of numbers was chosen because they are even more special than the Angel numbers. Not only have they been aged in fine old kegs, but they've also been treated with a durable polymer sealant that resists corrosion, cracking, and losses. And if you buy that, I may be willing to sell you the mineral rights to the valuable rhinestone deposits underneath my backyard, about sixty miles down.

Kidding aside, any group of twelve numbers *should* have the same performance expectation, but I have thoroughly tested this group, and I'm pleased with the results. So, I'm steering you in a direction that I have traveled, toward a wagering scheme that I can vouch for. But I'd like to add that I did similar experiments with other groups of twelve numbers. Result: a substantial reduction in my win rate. That should not have been the case, and yet it was. Perhaps my sampling was too small, but if you don't mind, I'd like to stick with the one that is a proven winner.

This betting configuration may look familiar to those readers who purchased my first book, *Gamble to Win,* because two-thirds of it is the Z bet from page 226 of that book. It covered the top two quad bets (shown here in Figure 22), and was called the Z because the shape of it resembles that letter. In subsequent studies, though, I learned that adding that third quad did remarkable things for the performance of the bet.

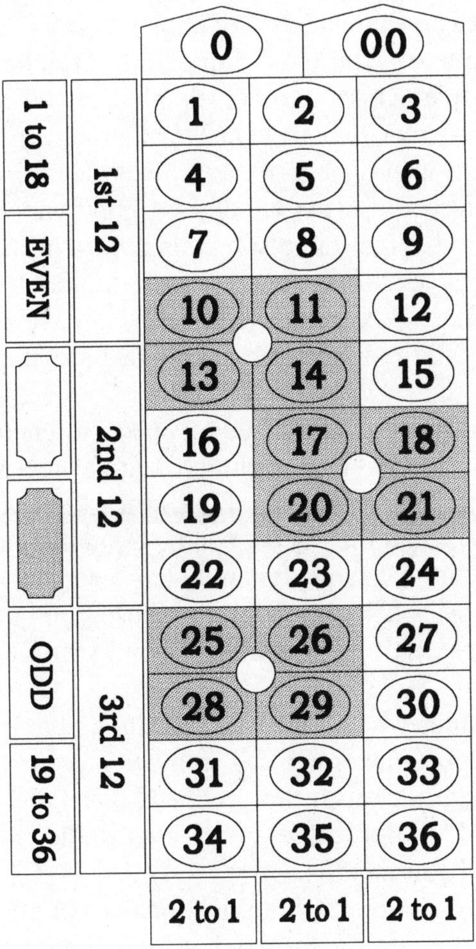

FIGURE 22
The 3Q Bet

The 3Q bet was born, and it has been a personal favorite of mine ever since.

I can't explain why this group of numbers seems to be more productive than any other group of twelve, if in fact that's the case, but it is my job to present gaming loopholes to my readers, and this one seems to be a fit. The most compelling argument may lie in how well it complements the other element of the 3Q/A strategy (which is covered in Chapter 11). Together, the two have been proven to perform well enough to neutralize the casino's statistical advantage in a series of tests, which is a good enough reason for me to lay claim to having found something extraordinary.

How is it played? First, let me say that the 3Q bet is a major component of the 3Q/A strategy. Until you have mastered that strategy and feel you're ready to branch out, I recommend that you avoid it.

I say this because, with all due respect, to encourage its use by those not fully trained is something like putting a loaded gun in the hands of a six-year-old, and telling him to go have some fun. What I'm saying is that the 3Q bet can be dynamite in the hands of a skilled player, but that same dynamite has a way of blowing up in the face of an unseasoned player, during those rare but unavoidable times when things don't go perfectly. (I hope I won't get strung up for saying that!)

For the record, what you're seeking is double hits on the 3Q group. So, the appearance of a 3Q number is your cue to start a two- or three-stage series on the group. If that fails, a new series can be launched at that table or another table, after the next appearance of a 3Q number.

That's not too hard, but complications can come up when you incorporate that bet into a formal betting scheme. You have to know what to do when you win, and when you lose.

And, when you lose, lose, lose.

Someone with experience playing this bet will know, from the table patterns, which way to go when arriving at the crossroads. And there's no substitute for experience, but ahead you will find some guidelines to help simulate the effect.

BET REGRESSIONS

To get the most from a table, one has to know how to regress. This is not difficult or complex, but it is something that is probably overlooked by many players.

A bet regression is part of the *press and pull* family. The best time to use a regression is when you're trying to hold onto most of the profit you have already accumulated, while attempting to get a little more.

Example: after just two minutes of play, you've reached your win goal. Since the wins came so easy, you think you might have hit a *wonder table:* one that keeps you winning interminably. You'd like to take advantage of the opportunity, but don't want to risk too much of what you've won. The solution: keep doing what you're doing, but with smaller bets.

This is how you keep (most of) your profit locked up while pursuing an enhanced goal.

Making money in casinos is like climbing a ladder. You want to go up one step at a time, and down one step at a time. The ones who don't make it go up one, and down fourteen. In other words, they can't handle their losses.

Every single minute you're at a table, you have to be aware of where you're at on the ladder, and how far you will fall if you should lose your footing. With each new bet, you're angling to make it to the next step. When a loss comes, you can't let it knock you down. You've got to hang on. Study that loss, and be prepared for the best and worst outcomes.

Bet regressions can help you maximize your gains, without putting your accrued profit at too much risk.

BET USAGE

Some readers may wonder if I play the bets I advocate, and if so, how often? The following chart shows my estimated bet usage at roulette, for the past year and beyond:

BET USAGE	
DESCRIPTION	PERCENT USED
ANGEL or 3Q	40%
TARGETED SIXLINES	15%
SLEDGEHAMMER	12%
SLEDGE B	8%
PATTERN BETS	5%
ODDBALL BETS	5%
EXPERIMENTAL BETS	15%

The Angel and the 3Q are currently my personal favorites. Targeted Sixlines are covered ahead in Chapter 13. The Sledge and Sledge B are frequently last resorts, when my primary strategy gets me into trouble. But those are only played for as long as they help me win, and I usually lay off after losing the first one. Pattern bets are employed when I'm battling back and spot an opportunity, like a P3 or a Reoccurring Double in its prime.

Oddball bets are random bets played in a limited way, usually after seeing a negative trend like the 1st 12, for example, not hitting for ten or more spins. In that case, I might venture a small two-stage series on the neglected area. Experimental bets, lastly, are part of my ongoing research.

10

SURGICAL STRIKES

Hit and Run. It is the only way you can consistently walk away with (the casino's) money.

—Lyle Stuart

The quote above sums up my feeling on how to make money in casinos. And this concurs with what I've said in all my books: Surgical Strikes are the best way to maintain a winning percentage as a player of casino table games.

Why is that? Because it's so damn easy to get sucked into playing their game. There is such a multitude of traps that spring open with every step you take and every moment you spend inside a casino. You don't stand a chance!

What am I talking about? It's about the enticing environment they offer, the girls, the alcohol, the chips, and the sights, sounds, and sensations of the casino.

It's about the fast pace of the games, with which you cannot compete. And the nonstop bets that give you no time to think. And the hypnotic effect of the wheel that never stops turning.

It's about your dire need to get back at the table for taking your money away. It's about the casino's statistical edge. It's about justice, fairness, and the cessation of mind control.

Look, man, it's simple. If you're going to play their game, don't surrender to *their* terms when you have the choice to do it on *your* terms. I know it all seems so warm and friendly and innocent, but good god, man, who do you think paid for the marble columns, and the carpeting, and the chandeliers?

They know, that if they can suck you into just forty minutes of play at a table game, you'll encounter patterns from the regular flow of the game that will throw you for a loop. That's when they get you. When statistical flukes land in the lap of the unprepared. Then you start changing your game plan to compensate. And then you have to change it yet again, to compensate for compensating. Before long, you're looking up from inside a hole that's forty feet deep, which in itself would not be so bad if only you were standing in something other than quicksand.

And that's just one of a thousand little snares they've set up for you. Did I say a thousand? I meant ten thousand.

To win, you've got to keep yourself detached from the game, and, the *effects* of the game. You can't accomplish that if you pull up a chair like you're sitting down to a game of checkers, just like all the other players whose lot in life is to lose.

So exactly what is a surgical strike? In military terms, it's *an offensive maneuver that strikes a target with pinpoint precision.* Through coordination of timing and position, you're hoping to hit a precise target, and only that target, and then make a quick retreat before the enemy can react.

Pearl Harbor, on December 7, 1941, is a fine example. There, the Japanese caught the U.S. military by surprise. The result was a stunning victory for Japan.

This is what you want to achieve in a casino, except that your weapons are your gaming chips, and you'll be seeking a monetary rather than military victory. How is it achieved? Through careful analysis of the table patterns beforehand, disciplined play during the session, and by exiting quickly, before the table has a chance to get back at you!

The execution of this concept takes all the fun out of playing casino table games, but that's the price of success.

THE APPLICATION OF RACETRACK WAGERING TECHNIQUES TO CASINO GAMES

Moving in silently, downwind and out of sight, you've got to strike when the moment is right, without thinking.

—Pink Floyd, from *Animals*

Recently, I was referred to an article about someone named Ernie Dahlman, who, according to the story, earns a pretax income of about $700,000 a year betting on thoroughbred horses at races simulcast from all over the country. He specializes in exotic bets like exacta and pick six. Since it was written by a *New York Times* staff writer who spent several days with him, my tendency is to believe that this is true.

I found the article to be something of an inspiration. I don't make $700K a year, but I see no reason why I couldn't, if it really meant that much to me. It's not a matter of not wanting the money; it's what I would have to put myself through to get it.

But I digress. Mr. Dahlman spends considerable time poring over statistics and other information, seeking a handful of targeted wagers a day. This is the surgical strike mentality.

This gives him an edge that few players could aspire to have, but the racetrack *takeout,* that is, the money deducted off the top from the wagering (which is used to pay the track's expenses), is a powerful disadvantage.

According to the aforementioned article, the New York State racing authorities dealt Mr. Dahlman a heavy setback several years ago, when they raised the takeout on exacta bets from 17 percent to 20 percent. That 3 percent difference represented a loss of about $300,000 a year to Dahlman.

If three percent can make that much difference, imagine the impact of paying only 5.26 percent (the house edge for roulette), instead of 17 percent or 20 percent. Wouldn't he make quite a bit more? Of course, he's dealing with the performance of trained athletes that have an established track record, which might be more predictable than the outcome of a roulette wheel that is precision-made to ensure a random result.

But working against him, is the fact that there is no sure-fire way to gauge the mood of a horse on a given day, versus the mood of the entire field that's running against him.

So, if you ask me, I would say that you're better off relying on the power of trends in a game with a 5 percent edge, than the disposition of an animal that is competing in a game that carries a 20 percent edge.

But this is beside the point. If you could simulate racetrack conditions—where you have to wait thirty minutes between betting opportunities—you can do what he did, with less penalty. That is, pretend you're at a racetrack instead of a casino, and pace your betting to achieve that effect. Confine your play to when the table is hot-wired to produce the results you seek, and your future could be very promising!

Now, you don't have to wait the full thirty minutes between bets. The point is simply to give yourself enough time to consider your best move at various points along the way, so that you don't end up chasing your tail.

Casinos love to see players chasing their tails! They are there to entertain *you*, but sometimes it works the other way around. But you don't go there to give them a show, do you?

So it comes down to this: you need to impose a pace that *you* control. This works best, however, when applied with the mentality that I refer to as *controlled greed*.

CONTROLLED GREED

Greed is good. Greed is right. Greed works.

—Gordon Gekko, from
the movie *Wall Street*

In the most compelling moment of the movie *Wall Street,* Gordon Gekko, echoing the words of Ivan Boesky, proclaimed at a stockholder's meeting that *greed is good.* But isn't greed one of the seven deadly sins? Isn't it the great destroyer of men who were legends, and some of the most brilliant minds in world history? Well, sure. But it has its place, if controlled.

Controlled greed? Greed used in moderation? Yep. Look at it as one of the many paradoxes of gaming, if you must, but I believe that it can be advantageous, when applied with the right mindset, to one's style of play.

To survive as a successful gambler, one needs an excess of ambition, and a touch of greed. You have to have the stomach for large bets, along with the good sense to quit at the right moment. You must desensitize yourself to the sums of money you're turning over, while you retain the underlying knowledge of how much those chips are worth.

You need a strong incentive to guide you past the temptations and the loneliness that will constantly envelop you and push you into the gratification vacuum that is part of this life. You will be in the no-man's land between seduction and discipline, and there will be no peace until you quit for the day.

It's what it takes to get you through it all.

APPLYING THE CONCEPTS

Your focus determines your reality.

—Qui Gon, from
Star Wars prequel

So, how is the *surgical strike* mentality coordinated with the concept of *controlled greed?*

You have to look at it almost as if it's a military engagement; a commando raid by an elite task force.

First, you scout the perimeter, looking for signs of positive or adverse playing conditions. What is the general feel? Is there room at the tables? Do all the roulette tables have electronic scoresigns? Are the table minimums reasonable?

As the situation comes into focus, you mentally prepare for the bets you will make, how much money to invest, what to say, when to leave. Then the countdown to the commencement of your attack may begin.

Your assignment is to seize, retain, and exploit the initiative. Before you send a single soldier (dollar) to engage your opponent (the house), you must have envisioned the full range of outcomes: full victory (winning with no resistance), partial victory (suffering interim losses), and defeat. This is a limited war in which no more will be risked than what you decided up front. There is no chance that you will be suckered into a prolonged war of attrition. You'll be out of there in a matter of minutes.

Your goals are reasonable, and attainable. You're not seeking a lucky win. You're there to drop in, strike, and retreat.

They'll never know what hit 'em.

THE SURGICAL SLEDGE

Some years ago, while at the Grand Victoria casino in Rising Sun, Indiana, my partner Sharon and I were getting ready to leave, after having an unproductive day. I was down exactly $100, which is not what I consider a serious loss, but of course there is no such thing as a pretty loss.

Know this: all losses hurt.

We were just about to exit when I decided to put down a bet at the roulette table by the door. Without looking at the scoresign, I pulled four quarters ($25 chips) from my hip pocket and covered the sledge numbers 7 through 30. That bet won, so I decided to try it one more time. Another winner. Immediately, we left. I was pleased to have erased our deficit in the space of less than two minutes. I had to pay for the buffet (afterwards) out of my pocket, but I felt much better, knowing I had dodged a loss.

Shrewd bet, or impulsive bet? When they win, it's tempting to say it was a smart bet. When they lose, well, it's just another example of a fool and his money.

This bet is not recommended as an automatic response to having a bad session. It is a salve which must be used sparingly, for it loses its potency if it's overused. On the basis described, I think it can be classified as a smart bet. But used indiscriminately, it's a quick trip to the loser's arcade.

At that time, I had been keeping a running count of how my sledge bets were doing, and I knew I was due to win some. Now, I know how that must sound, expecting to win a bet (no matter what casino I was in), based on the results of previous bets elsewhere. But that's how the statistics seem to play out.

This is part of the surgical strike mindset: becoming familiar with the win rate of your key bets, and maintaining a mental tally of how they are doing. After you've done this a while, you develop an instinct for when to bet, based on subconscious knowledge that you may not have known you had!

For those who don't have this databank of information, there is a way to qualify a table for the surgical sledge. First, you want to avoid tables where the scoresign shows a lot of zeroes. Next, look at the pattern of the numbers. Are the sledge and angel numbers coming up in groups, or are they interspersed? What you want is for the two groups to be segregated.

If the table meets these two conditions, you may have found a table that qualifies for one or two bets.

Another time when I am prone to use the surgical sledge is to help me battle back from a losing session of some other strategy. Example: I'm playing the 3Q/A, and my bets aren't firing, to the point where I've reached my loss limit. This means I have to quit. But then I look at the pattern, and realize that a sledge bet would probably be a good fit at that table. So I cheat. I tell myself that the loss limit applied to the 3Q/A, and that a small experiment with another strategy would be allowable.

Of course, this is a shameless rationalization. You see that, don't you? And I'm supposed to be teaching you the proper moves. But the sad truth is that it's very unlikely that you're going to do everything by the book, anyway, even if you put out a determined effort to do so. Because, no plan works for everyone. Eventually, it gets customized to our individual styles.

In my case, I give myself license to bend the rules in certain situations. If it works, it becomes an adaptation rather than a lapse of discipline. But in dealing with the surgical sledge, this can get tricky. If you lose two or three of these bets (tops!), then forget it. Acknowledge that it's not helping.

Hmmm. It seems that in my effort to try to fill the page with words after I had finished saying what I wanted to say, I ended up philosophizing about styles of play.

But you were onto that even before my admission, right?

THE SURGICAL ANGEL

The surgical angel is a simple, straightforward bet. All you're seeking is a table (with a scoresign) where an angel number was the last one to win, under these conditions:

1) Prior to that, the last two (or more) table decisions were won by sledgehammer numbers.
2) Preceding the above, the table had showed a tendency to produce angel numbers in groups of two or more.

Such a table is ripe for a surgical angel bet. Play a two-bet series and then, if that didn't produce a win, move on. If it wins one of those bets, this also is your cue to move on.

Remember, if anyone else is using value chips for inside bets, you may have to have your value chips converted to table chips for the duration of your stay at that table.

THE SURGICAL 3Q

This is even more simple than the surgical angel. At a table where you see 3Q numbers coming up in groups, wait for a gap in the 3Q numbers, followed by a single 3Q number.

That's your cue to commence a wagering series like above, where you leave after one win or two losses. Then rinse, shampoo and repeat at another table.

FIXED SPLITS

You can't expect to hit the jackpot if you don't put a few nickels in the machine.

—Flip Wilson

One thing you should have in your bag of tricks is a strategy that is *incrementally correct:* one that meshes perfectly with the table minimums, by virtue of unit levels that are divisible by five. Such is the case with *fixed splits.*

This type of bet came to my attention about seven years ago, when I noticed an Asian chap walking up to my table and playing nickels on five numbers for a few bets before moving on. He did this twice, making $200 or so at each table. To this day I wonder what his wagering trigger was, for he seemed to know in advance what results the table would produce.

Be that as it may, I found myself imitating what he did, as an experiment, which proved successful. Nowadays, I play it on those occasions when I need a fill-in bet in $5 increments, to help hold my spot at the table.

Fixed Splits, as I call it, is a bet that is formed by putting five chips on a set group of split bets. The numbers I have chosen are 10–13, 17–20, 26–29, 33–36 and 0–00, which are the numbers the Asian man chose, if memory serves. Individually, each bet pays 17–1, but collectively they form a 5–2 payoff, which is halfway between 2–1 and 3–1.

A total of ten numbers are covered, and six of those are part of the 3Q bet, which as you know is a favorite of mine. Figure 23 shows the coverage of this bet.

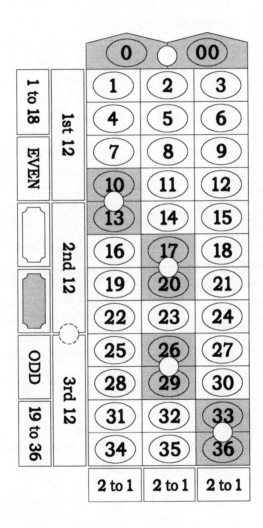

FIGURE 23
Fixed Split Locations

A specific betting trigger hasn't been established for this bet. It is intended to be used, like I said, as a fill-in bet to hold your seat while awaiting a table condition for something else you're playing. But I wouldn't recommend playing it unless you have noticed that numbers from this group are hitting.

Some readers, who like the 5–2 payoff, may wish to devise a strategy of their own based around these numbers, or the general concept. I see no reason to discourage this, as long as some testing has been done beforehand, using previously recorded roulette table results, or a published system tester.

Speaking of system testers, I have found the 7,140 numbers that are printed in the back of Frank Scoblete's book, *Spin Roulette Gold,* to be the best system tester on the market for surgical strikes. It is even better than the 15,000 table results in Erick St. Germain's *Roulette System Tester,* because it's broken down into 357 sessions of 20 each, as opposed to 15 sessions of 1000 each. The former will more correctly simulate short term play at numerous tables, which is how surgical strikes are played.

For the record, in the table results from *Spin Roulette Gold,* there was one column (of 357) that showed no fixed split numbers whatsoever, and three columns had just one number. All others had two or more. The most fixed split numbers in any column was fourteen (out of twenty), which occurred in the fourth column of page 171. That column has been reprinted on the following page (with permission from the publisher) to give you an idea how the numbers can play out (in the extreme).

One thing in particular that I like about playing fixed splits is the fact that the 0 and 00 are part of the bet. Here, they do not serve as a hedge, but instead, are just two more numbers out of the ten that are covered.

The reason I like this is, I suppose, a matter of professional pride. I don't like being caught with my pants down, but that's how I feel whenever a zero wins and I didn't cover it. It is nothing more than vanity on my part to want to be seen as someone who didn't overlook that bet, but as a player who is supposedly an expert in these matters, I have an image to preserve!

0	Fixed Split No.
18	
26	Fixed Split No.
3	
0	Fixed Split No.
13	Fixed Split No.
00	Fixed Split No.
8	
13	Fixed Split No.
36	Fixed Split No.
16	
26	Fixed Split No.
7	
22	
26	Fixed Split No.
36	Fixed Split No.
29	Fixed Split No.
20	Fixed Split No.
33	Fixed Split No.
0	Fixed Split No.

FIGURE 24
Sample Fixed Split Numbers
Numbers reprinted from fourth column, page 171

Now don't be deceived; this is an extraordinary run of fixed split numbers, which happened only once out of 357 trials. Most of the time, you'll see perhaps three to five numbers from this group within every set of twenty numbers.

If you see a pattern of these selected numbers on the roulette scoresign, it might not be a bad idea to venture a series, especially when there are a lot of zeroes showing.

MIXED MEDIA

In lieu of playing fixed splits while your engine is idling at the tables, there is a technique for playing outside bets. I call this group of bets *mixed media,* because you have twelve types of bets from which to choose.

The essence of mixed media is to go after a betting target that appears to be statistically overdue. In looking things over, check both the even money bets and the 2–1 bets. The question you want to ask yourself is: which bet type (if any) looks like it is out of step with the probabilities?

For example, you may have observed that no numbers from the first dozen have won in the last twelve or fifteen spins. So, as long as you're in a holding mode, why not venture a small wager on the 1st 12? If it wins, you've done a good deed. If it loses, then you have to make a judgment call: do you want to invest one more bet, or abandon the chase?

The key to success, here, is to keep things in perspective. Remember: you didn't come here to play that bet. It's just a fill-in. So, not only should it be a very small bet, but you must never, ever chase it if you lose. A small bet or two, and that's it. Win or lose, you forget about that bet and seek a new target, or get back to what you were originally doing.

The 2–1 bets can be lucrative (in a small-time kind of way) when they're firing, but most of my mainstay activity of this sort is in the form of even money bets. Another example that could apply to the above situation is to choose 1–18 as your target instead of 1st 12. This has a smaller payoff, but offers six more ways to win. A pretty solid bet, under the circumstances.

Those are two of the twelve possibilities. There is also Even, Odd, Red, Black, 2nd column, 3rd 12, etc. Most of the time, I use pattern play, with even money bets, seeking out an opportunity to exploit a reoccurring single or double with Red or Black. These are easy to spot, since the scoresigns tell you at a glance when there's something afoot. Even (most of) the online casinos have a record of the last ten or twenty numbers displayed, broken down into the Red or Black categories.

There will always be times, however, when you need a fill-in bet but nothing is going on. And, you are committed to place a bet. In those cases, you can do one of two things. Look for the most likely prospect out of the meager offerings, or *go to Red*. That's a favorite bet of mine in such situations. It means, when in doubt, bet on Red. It's a bet which can be surprisingly effective, considering the level of desperation that's involved!

The main thing you want to be looking for is an imbalance of some kind. If you don't see anything good, ask yourself: are the odd and even bets showing even the slightest favoritism? If so, bet on the opposite choice. What about high or low? In some cases, you may have noticed an encompassing trend, where Red or Black is dominating, and you would like to pursue the dominant trend. This is the opposite of what I'm suggesting here, but you have to look at the picture from all sides.

Of course, even if you're in a land casino and are obligated to bet every spin, you can always appear to be deep in thought, then glance at the dealer and gesture to the effect that you want to pass this spin. As long as you don't overdo it, and there are other players at the table, this is always an option.

A final tip: don't forget about the fixed splits bet, if suddenly you find that the zeroes are making an entrance. This turn of events will always come up from time to time, so don't forget about that choice, when it looks to be a fit.

AUXILIARY BETS

There will be times—while in pursuit of a set goal—when it comes to your attention that an unusual table pattern is emerging. This is the kind of betting opportunity that doesn't come up often, and you'd like to take advantage of it. But this poses a dilemma: would this not compromise the discipline that is a vital part of one's success in this endeavor?

Example: while awaiting the wagering trigger for a certain strategy, you notice a classic reoccurring double coming into play. You just want to make one or two bets, but you think this might be in conflict with your original objective.

It is important that one doesn't get distracted from one's goal, and not forget that the casinos are masters of distraction. Does this then mean that one has to shrug off these opportunities as being untouchable, every time?

Not necessarily. As long as you keep matters in perspective, there is a way to handle these situations: auxiliary bets. Bets that are made from a separate fund that has been established explicitly for that purpose. But this fund should be much smaller than your original buy-in, and closely monitored.

In the above example, you would make a decision as to how much you are willing to invest in this effort, and put aside just as many chips as you need for that purpose. This fund should be no greater than 20% of your earlier buy-in. Then, keep a close watch on how these side bets are doing. And, be sure to put an asterisk on that line of your scorecard, to identify it.

If you're not seeing instant results, acknowledge that it was not the opportunity you thought it was, and bail out!

THE SIGNATURE BET

An offshoot of the auxiliary bet is the signature bet. That is, a pet wager that you make whenever seeing a certain table condition. While it may appear to be an impulse bet (to the untrained eye), it is nothing of the sort, because the decision to proceed with it was made long before you arrived at the table.

An example of a signature bet would be to bet the 3rd Dozen whenever you pass a table where a number from that group has just won the last decision. Personally, I prefer the Angel or 3Q for such bets, but I'm suggesting the 3rd Dozen because it's easier to reach, and, being an outside bet, you shouldn't have to be concerned with other players using value chips.

Another type of signature bet is technically a group of bets. Example: you could commence a three-stage series on the zeroes whenever you pass a table where a zero just won. Lord knows, the green monsters frequently travel in packs. This could position you to cash in on some 17–1 returns!

Ideally, the performance of these wagers should be tracked on the *statistics scorecard* (coming up), because in my experience, groups of random bet results start to concur with the statistics after thirty or forty trials. So, if my records reveal that these bets are overperforming, I prepare myself for the inevitable compensatory losing streak (by betting smaller). And if these side bets have been underperforming, I get ready to harvest some wins. I have an edge, because I have a clue as to what to expect.

Just a thought. A way to make the drudgery of living a life surrounded by numbers a little more bearable. Wouldn't hurt to try to impose a tiny bit of fun!

11

ALL ABOUT THE 3Q/A REVERSE SELECT

Despite the fact that the 3Q/A—as presented here—is in the surgical strike class, I have opted to devote this entire chapter to it, since there is a lot of ground to cover.

The 3Q/A is the centerpiece strategy of this book. It's the one that I believe can overcome the casino's statistical advantage, as no wagering scheme for roulette ever has in the past. It is the result of a great deal of research on my part, and I am pleased to be able to present it to the public for the first time.

Here's a little surprise: we've already covered all the betting components of this strategy. The only thing you need to know is how to combine the elements.

Bet-wise, there are two components involved: the 3Q bet and the Angel bet, which has been abbreviated to "A". Together, they form the *3Q/A Reverse Select.* But there are a few little twists that make this one different from anything else presented in this book. For one thing, the table has to be qualified, a process that requires you to hold out for a certain table condition. Fortunately, in most cases, this involves nothing more than a quick glance at the last five table decisions.

126

THE 3Q/A REVERSE SELECT

One thing that helped this bet evolve is the way *Intercasino* (online casino) shows the last five table decisions on a simulated scoresign at the start of play.* Since most of my play these days is online, I've revised my customized scorecard (see Chapter 12) to show up to five pre-session spins at the top.

Making note of the five previous spins of the roulette wheel is a big part of what contributes to the success of the 3Q/A Reverse Select. This is where the choice of which strategy (the 3Q or the A) is made, and that's what makes it work so well.

What you're looking for during the preliminary 5-spin period is which of the two bet types forms a majority. For example, if the first five numbers are 16–4–22–0–19, then the 'A' group qualifies, because there is one angel (A) number, and no 3Q numbers. Once you've done that, you select the other group (3Q) as your wagering target for that session. The name 3Q/A Reverse Select comes from targeting the opposite of the dominant table trend.

After that, there is the elimination step: if the target had back-to-back wins in the qualification period, that table is disqualified (since the trend you're seeking has come and gone).

If five spins are insufficient to establish a majority, you will have to wait until the next 3Q or A number wins. When it does, choose the opposite category of the number breaking the deadlock, then go through the elimination step. After that, you must wait for the appearance of a number from the group, then you start a series, which ends after: 1) a win, or 2) three consecutive losses.

*I later learned that those five numbers (and only those five) are not valid. (See pages 144, 168, and 172 for clarification.)

If you lose that series, wait for another appearance of your wagering trigger, and then launch one more series. If you can't nab a win after playing two series, leave the table.

Let's review the steps:

1) From the last five roulette table decisions, seek a majority of numbers from either the A or the 3Q group (illustrated in Figures 18 and 22, on pages 98 and 105).
2) If there was a majority from the five spins, your wagering target will be the *other* (minority) group.
3) If there is no majority between the two groups, continue reviewing table results. When a number from one group wins, that certifies the *other* group as the target.
4) In either case, a series should not be started until the next appearance of a number from the selected group.
5) Before starting a series, confirm that no numbers from the chosen group came up consecutively during qualification. If it did, that table is disqualified.
6) When a number from the targeted group appears, launch a three-bet series on that group immediately.
7) If the fifth qualifying number is from the targeted group, and was not immediately preceded by another number from that group, use it as the wagering trigger.
8) If your first series loses, stop betting until another number from the targeted group comes up, which is the trigger to begin a second (three-bet) series.
9) Note: a second series shall be enacted *only* if you lost all three bets from the first series.
10) Stop betting and leave the table after either a win occurs, or both series have been exhausted.
11) Continue on that basis at other tables, as desired.

This, of course, tells you what and when to bet, but not how much to bet at the various stages of play. Meaning, what kind of bet fluctuations are called for after a win, after a loss, and after a series of losses. We'll get to that shortly.

In the meantime, you need to become familiar with examples of this procedure. For this, arrangements were made for reprinting selected columns of numbers from another book, which have also served, in part, to help validate this strategy.

The book chosen for verifying the win rate of the 3Q/A is Frank Scoblete's *Spin Roulette Gold,* by Bonus Books. This was picked because it contains 7140 roulette spins—in groups of 20— that were copied from scoresigns in Las Vegas and Atlantic City. On that basis, the group simulates 357 live sessions, each of which is just about the perfect length to conclude a wagering series for a (surgical strike) type of bet such as this.

One might think that the 15,000 table results offered in Erick St. Germain's *Roulette System Tester* would provide an even better testing ground, but this is not the case. In that book, the results are broken down into just 15 sessions of 1000 spins apiece. So, we end up choosing between 15 sessions that are much too long, or 357 sessions that are an ideal length.

But this raises the question: since each page of St. Germain's book contains 60 spins, couldn't each page be treated as a new session? Nope. This doesn't offer the diversity of results that come from the (nomadic) surgical strike technique, which is necessary to ensure the effectiveness of this procedure.

To satisfy my curiosity, however, some tests of that nature were made. The results indicated that trends favoring or opposing the 3Q/A strategy can hang on for hundreds of spins! Meaning, if a table starts out bad, it can stay bad for a long time. This may defy logic, but it's one of the realities of gaming that one must accept. And *that* is why you have to keep moving.

The statistics from these trials are documented ahead in this chapter, so you can see how the numbers play out.

Let us now look at a few sample trials. In *Spin Roulette Gold,* the main testing medium used, each page contains 7 columns of 20 numbers on the top half of the page, and another 7 columns on the bottom half of the page. The following are the first two columns, top and bottom, on page 150, which is the first page of the system tester numbers offered in that book:

Column 1, top		Column 1, bottom		Column 2, top		Column 2, bottom	
25		34		14		2	
29		35		1		30	
2		0		34		2	
29		1		34		36	
25	____A	18	____3Q	30	____3Q	36	____3Q
36		25	W	2		17	
16	L	10		0		17	W
10	L	4		30		19	
2	W	2		12		11	
8		3		26		15	
5		26		4	L	36	
22		29		17	W	0	
29		36		4		20	
27		25		21		3	
12		13		18		10	
16		31		35		14	
3		35		11		21	
23		5		24		23	
14		24		32		33	
33		14		11		00	

FIGURE 25
Four Sample Columns
Numbers reprinted from page 150,
Spin Roulette Gold

Not a bad start. Four wins and three losses from a bet that pays 2–1. If you were playing with hundred dollar chips, you would have made $1500* from those seven bets. But please don't be carried away by my idle speculation, since this group is not a typical representative sampling.

*Computing the return from using $100 chips is more complicated than multiplying 7 bets times 4 wins, because the A bet uses two units (chips), and the 3Q uses three units, for each bet.

Do you understand the markings in Figure 25? The first thing you do, is draw a line after the fifth number. All those north of that line are the qualifying numbers.

In the first column, the qualifying numbers contain four 3Qs and an A. Since A is from the minority group, A will be our target. So, we write the letter A in the vicinity of the line we drew. Then, we have to wait for an A number to appear. That happens on the sixth line, so we launch a betting series. We lose the first two bets, but catch a win at the third stage.

The second column has three As and one 3Q number in the qualification group, so 3Q is our choice. Notice that the last of the five qualifying numbers is a 3Q number, and it wasn't preceded by another 3Q number. This meets the requirements of rule number 7, from page 128, which means no waiting, so we can begin a series without delay. We do, and win the first bet. What do we do next? Rule Number 10: leave the table.

I would like to take a moment to express the importance of strict adherence to Rule Number 10. Win or lose, you gotta to keep moving. Not only does this help you keep your edge, but it doesn't serve your interests to stay in one place. Good trends tend to fade, and the bad trends tend to hang on forever. And you never know what you're getting until it's over.

The third column shown also has three As and one 3Q. But it takes a while for a 3Q number to show. That occurs on line 10, so we start a series, sustaining a loss on our first bet, and then hitting a winner on the second, on line 12.

The last column has four As and no 3Qs at all, so once again, 3Q is the choice. Our trigger shows up on the sixth line, so we start a series and win on the first try. That's one thing I like about the 3Q/A: I seem to catch a lot of easy wins.

Obviously, one of your key decisions will be which brand of wheelbarrow you should get to carry away all the loot you'll earn. I recommend the Rodeo Flyer 900. But it's self-propelled, so don't let it get away from you! It's no fun chasing after a motorized cart that's carrying your money away. (I've spoken to the manufacturer about this glaring design flaw.)

Now, let's look at some unique situations:

Page 158: column 4, top		Page 159: column 5, bottom		Page 160: column 1, top		Page 160: column 2, top	
18		10		0		00	
7		27		14		11	
36		0		0		26	
33		20		16		36	
12	___3Q	21	___A	1	___	6	___
24		1		28	___A	7	
2		15	L	3		27	
19		8	L	34	W	13	
5		20	L	10		11	
15		17		3		21	
31		25		22		15	
15	**Non-**	12		26		16	**Disqualified**
16	**Playable**	20		7		5	
30		30		23		2	
5		26		28		24	
15		2		2		17	
9		29	L	32		1	
31		1	W	28		29	
9		23		10		1	
14		1		5		17	

FIGURE 26
Four Sample Columns
Numbers reprinted from pages 158, 159 & 160

In the first column above, we established the wagering target, but there was insufficient table data to complete a session. (Eleven of the 357 sessions were thus affected.)

The second column shows a session that squeaked by with a win on the second bet of the last series, after a period where the player had to sit through seven spins while waiting for the new wagering trigger to present itself.

Rarely do you have to wait so long to get a chance to bet, but it occasionally happens. In such a case, you may need to consider some *mixed media* options to hold your seat.

The last two columns illustrate what happens when the five qualifying numbers are insufficient to establish a majority between the two bet categories. In the first of these two columns, there was only one A and 3Q (apiece)—within the five qualifying numbers. Fortunately, the next spin produced a 3Q number, which clears the path for choosing A as the wagering target. We draw a second line below the first line, and write the wagering target (A) at the end of the line, as a reminder of the category we're pursuing. On the next spin an A number comes up, so we bet the A, and win the first bet when another A number comes right up.

The last column shows another deadlock: two 3Q numbers (11 and 26) and two A numbers (36 and 6). Ah, but a closer look at the group reveals that both categories were victims of back-to-back hits, which calls Rule Number 5 (from page 128) into play. That rule states that when numbers from the category you're pursuing had back-to-back hits in the qualification period, that table must be disqualified. And since this is the case with both categories (in this instance), there is no need to look further.

This should be all you need to know to establish the wagering target, and when to bet on what. Ahead, we will cover the specific bet amounts for typical and non-typical series.

By the way, it might not be a bad idea to purchase a copy of Frank Scoblete's *Spin Roulette Gold,* so you can copy the numbers that were used as a system verifier for the 3Q/A, and see what kind of win and loss streaks are likely to come up. It never hurts to have a clear picture of what you're getting into.

Unless. . .you've chosen to jump into a volcano. In that case, I would recommend that you *close* your eyes, and be sure to wear a polyester suit! (Thus, there will be one less of *those* in the world.) But this advice applies only to those who are deeply committed to sacrificing their lives for an idiotic ritual.

I really can't get behind this volcano thing. Surely there's a better way to deal with one's problems.

3Q/A STATISTICS

At the end of all 357 sessions, the player side wound up with a 30.5-bet advantage over the house. Sounds like a pretty slim lead to end up with after roughly three weeks of work, doesn't it? Well, that result is based on flat bets. You can do better than that with a fluctuating wagering structure. Also, don't forget that since these are 2–1 bets, twice that many bets (61) could have been lost, and the house would still have no statistical edge over the player. To give you a sense of what's possible, however, let's first look at what you could earn from flat bets of $100.

With flat $100 bets throughout, 30½ wins at 2–1 will earn a pre-tax income of $6100, which works out to about $2000 a week. But this is only theoretical, because $100 bets aren't really possible with both sides of this bet. The A side is no problem: two quarters on each sixline makes a $100 bet. The 3Q, however, would require $33⅓ on each of the three quads to form a $100 bet, and we all know that isn't exactly possible.

For simplicity, let's use $60 as the total bet amount, which works for both sides. This would earn $3660, or, $1220 a week, if you play fifteen to twenty sessions a day.

Now, there was some statistical variance to deal with. At the high point (session 336), the player advantage was 35.5 bets over 0% house edge, which would have earned $4260 at the $60 level, if you stopped there. It's a bit discouraging to find out that the last twenty-one sessions were spent losing one-seventh of the money you had accumulated, isn't it?

That's the way it is in the real world of successful gambling. All that matters is that you show a profit at the end.

What about the low end of the statistical variance? Not bad. There were only five sessions (all within the first eighteen) where the house held an advantage. At its worst point, the house edge was just 1 bet over zero. But after that the player advantage kicked in, and the house never regained the lead.

So far (to give you baseline information), all we've talked about is flat bets. These are the safest types of bets, but they are not terribly efficient. You have to bet large, and tolerate long runs of mediocre performance. To get the most from your wagering efforts you need to fluctuate your bets. But when, and how?

As much as I'd like to lay it all out for you, different people are going to want to do it different ways. Some will be determined to go up-as-you-lose; others will want to do the opposite of that. Some will prefer a freestyle approach, while others will want to incorporate some kind of system.

Perhaps the best solution to this riddle is to show the statistics from these trials, so you can see for yourself what you're dealing with, in terms of the losing streaks, the win percentage, how many times the 0s came up, etc. After that, I'll make recommendations, from which you can choose.

STATISTICS:
Roulette trials, using Frank Scoblete's *Spin Roulette Gold:*

Number of Bets: 845
Number of Wins: 302
Number of Losses: 543
Final Win Percentage: 35.74%
0% House Edge (reference): 33.33%

Total number of Sessions: 357
Disqualified Sessions: 23
Non-Playable Sessions: 11
Total Played Sessions: 323
Number of Winning Sessions: 302
Number of Losing Sessions: 21

Session Win Percentage: 93.50%
Highest Player Advantage: 35.5 Bets over 0% house edge
Highest Player Disadvantage: 1 Bet under 0% house edge

Number of Sessions with Statistical Player Edge: 315
Number of Sessions with Statistical House Edge: 5
Number of Sessions with 0% Player Edge (Even): 3

Longest Losing Streaks (Bets): 10^2, 9^3, 8^6, 7^5, 6^5
    Note: Superscript indicates how many times (typical)
Longest Winning Streaks (Bets): 5^3, 4^4, 3^{19}

Longest Losing Streaks (Sessions): 1^{21}
Longest Winning Streaks (Sessions): 54^1, 39^1, 29^1, 22^1, 19^1,
    18^1, 17^1, 14^1, 12^1, 11^2, 10^1
Player Edge at end of all Sessions: 30.5 Bets over 0% Edge
Statistical Player Edge (over House) for entire group: 7.22%

Number of Losses to 0 or 00: 47 (5.56%)

The above information can be invaluable to someone who knows how to use it. But a great many readers will need for it to be interpreted.

Perhaps the most vital piece of information is the statistical player edge overall, which is 7.22%. That tells you that you're working with something that offers a strong chance to win. Next in importance are the losing streaks, for sessions and for bets. You need to know the extent of the probable downside.

According to the above, the longest losing streak for bets was 10, which happened only twice over a span of 845 bets. Then there were three occasions of nine consecutive losing bets, and six times when eight bets in a row lost. If you apply some kind of system, make sure that it can handle these strings of losses.

Also, make sure you can handle a streak of 54 consecutive *winning* sessions, as noted above!

Regarding session statistics, let's look at the losing streaks. Well, now, this is encouraging: there was never a time when two sessions lost consecutively. That doesn't mean it won't happen, but it's certainly a good sign.

It wouldn't hurt to study all the streaks, for bets and sessions, to familiarize yourself with what might be possible at both ends of the spectrum.

But there is still one piece of information that is missing: how does the 3Q/A perform at the various points along the way? Where do things stand after, say, every four out of the twenty-six pages that were used for system verification?

The following is that breakdown:

Page	Wins	Losses	Bets Over 0% House Edge
151	26	42	5 over
155	72	120	12 over
159	119	217	10.5 over
163	164	292	18 over
167	212	379	22.5 over
171	261	464	29 over
175	302	543	30.5 over

FIGURE 27
Periodic Status of 3Q/A

Figure 27 shows a general pattern where the player's edge is seeking its own level. Since every statistic—except one—shows an increase in the player advantage from the one before, more trials could push the end figure even higher.

Although this group of results is not a large enough sampling to irrefutably prove the 3Q/A success rate, the evidence does offer a positive indication. It wouldn't surprise me if the 7.22% player's edge slipped below 7% after several thousand more trials, but that would nevertheless mean that one might expect to reap a profit of $7 or so for every $100 wagered with flat bets, in much the same way that a casino makes *its* money!

For reference, the following shows the 3Q/A statistics for the *Roulette System Tester* by Erick St. Germain. In this study, there were only fifteen sessions, so these figures, though fantastic, aren't nearly as reliable as those of the previous study.

STATISTICS:
Roulette trials, using Erick St. Germain's *Roulette System Tester,* ©1995 by Zumma Publishing Company, Arlington, Texas:

Number of Bets: 36
Number of Wins: 15
Number of Losses: 21
Final Win Percentage: 41.67%
0% house edge (reference): 33.33%

Total number of Sessions: 15
Disqualified Sessions: 0
Non-Playable Sessions: 0
Total Played Sessions: 15
Number of Winning Sessions: 15
Number of Losing Sessions: 0

Longest Losing Streaks (Bets): 3^3, 2^4
Longest Winning Streaks (Bets): 2^4

Longest Losing Streaks (Sessions): 0
Longest Winning Streaks (Sessions): 15^1

Session Win Percentage: 100%
Final Statistical Player Edge (over House): 25.00%

Since there were only 15 playable sessions (without bending the rules of engagement for surgical strikes), there is no point in showing the comprehensive statistics that I felt were necessary for the last set of trials. But I wanted to be able to say that this well-known system tester was not overlooked.

3Q/A BETTING OPTIONS

In our quest to find a viable betting scheme for the 3Q/A, let's look at what can be accomplished with two tiers of flat bets: the first at or near the minimum level; the second twice that size. For this, we'll say that the five-spin analysis has established 3Q as the target. This is a three-unit bet, so we'll place $2 on each quad (forming a $6 bet) for the first series. If a second series is needed, we'll put $4 on each quad ($12 total):

SERIES	STAGE	BET	COST	WIN	PROFIT
	1	$6	$6	$12	$12
1	2	$6	$12	$12	$6
	3	$6	$18	$12	$0
	1	$12	$30	$24	$6
2	2	$12	$42	$24	–$6
	3	$12	$54	$24	–$18

FIGURE 28
3Q Series, Flat Bets

The first column (above) shows the series; the second shows the stages of each series; the third is the bet amount at each stage; the fourth is the cumulative cost; the fifth is the bet return; the last column is the profit. The figures shown at each new stage assume that all previous bets lost, and reflects the profit after those losses have been calculated in to the totals.

As the chart shows, we're better off if we catch the win in the first four bets. The point of the second series, however, is to give the player another shot at bringing in a win.

Let's take a look at an alternative that would offer roughly the same return, regardless the stage where the win occurs:

SERIES	STAGE	BET	COST	WIN	PROFIT
	1	$6	$6	$12	$12
1	2	$9	$15	$18	$12
	3	$12	$27	$24	$9
	1	$18	$45	$36	$9
2	2	$27	$72	$54	$9
	3	$42	**$114**	$84	$12

FIGURE 29
3Q Series, Fluctuating Bets

Here, the bet starts out the same, but has built-in increases each step of the way. This allows one to get a more even return from each stage, but you may have noticed that it costs roughly twice as much as the previous structure.

The figure below shows the betting equivalent for the above, as it pertains to the A bet:

SERIES	STAGE	BET	COST	WIN	PROFIT
	1	$6	$6	$12	$12
1	2	$8	$14	$16	$10
	3	$12	$26	$24	$10
	1	$18	$44	$36	$10
2	2	$28	$72	$56	$12
	3	$42	**$114**	$84	$12

FIGURE 30
A Series, Fluctuating Bets

Since this is a two-unit bet (as opposed to three), we're able to get a return that is more even throughout the stages. But the problem with these last two figures is that they get expensive in the latter stages. Isn't there something better?

What I recommend is to think of each series separately, using the configuration illustrated below. More important than making money at each stage is: *keeping your ass in the game.* The addition of the second series does that, by cutting down the losing sessions, since, at three out of four tables, if you don't win the first series, you'll win the second.

The overall cost of both series shown below ($81) is about midway between those of the previous examples.

SERIES	STAGE	BET	COST	WIN	PROFIT
	1	$6	$6	$12	$12
1	2	$9	$15	$18	$12
	3	$12	**$27**	$24	$9

SERIES	STAGE	BET	COST	WIN	PROFIT
	1	$12	$12	$24	$24
2	2	$18	$30	$36	$24
	3	$24	**$54**	$48	$18

FIGURE 31
Recommended 3Q Series

The formula for Figure 31 should be easy to remember. The bet amount for the first stage of series #2 matches that of the last stage of series #1. And, all bets in the second series are exactly double the size of the bets in the first series.

Please do not be misled; the profit figures in the second stage of Figure 31 do not factor in the money lost from the first series. But we're talking losses of just $3 in each of the first two stages, and $9 in the third. You should be able to cover that loss—and then some—in the very next session. From there, it's nothing but onward and upward.

This approach strikes a balance between maximizing your profit potential of a winning session, and the monetary outflow that is an unavoidable part of a losing session. One must keep an eye on both possibilities.

Figure 32 shows the recommendation for the two series with the A bet. Because of the adjustments in the bet amounts that are necessary when going from a three-unit bet to two units, this pair of series costs $3 less:

SERIES	STAGE	BET	COST	WIN	PROFIT
	1	$6	$6	$12	$12
1	2	$8	$14	$16	$10
	3	$12	**$26**	$24	$10

SERIES	STAGE	BET	COST	WIN	PROFIT
	1	$12	$12	$24	$24
2	2	$16	$28	$32	$20
	3	$24	**$52**	$48	$20

FIGURE 32
Recommended A Series

Figures 31 and 32 show my betting recommendations for the A and 3Q, playing at a $5 table. Losing a session will cost either $78 (for the A) or $81 (for the 3Q), but statistically, you should win 14 out of every 15 sessions.

Another way to go is to use flat bets exclusively, and let the 7.22% win rate grind out your profit. If that figure is accurate to within a percentage point or so (as I believe it is), you should be able to reap an average profit of $6 or $7 for every $100 wagered. It's an unimaginative way to play, but it should work, and doing it that way would certainly simplify things.

If you try that approach, though, you must learn to rise above the *I have to win today* mindset. You must treat wins and losses as raw numbers that are being processed on a factory assembly line. This removes the glory from the wins, but it also shields you from the pain of losing.

You have to look at it like this: wouldn't you rather spend two hours a day processing numbers for $1000 a week, than work eight hours a day for a substandard wage?

Now that you've seen an overview of betting options within a session, we need to look at the structure of bets from one session to the next.

As you have just read, I advocate either flat bets, or increases after a loss, or a merging of the two concepts, within a session. But going from session to session can be tricky. When playing such a costly bet, you have to be wary of the up-as-you-lose approach, unless you have the bankroll and the fortitude to ride out two or three consecutive losing sessions. A scenario like that won't come up often, but if you play long enough, it'll happen. If your increase is very slight, though, like starting a series with an $8 bet (for A) instead of $6, and, you regress immediately after you recoup the money lost, you might do all right.

What if you try that, and lose the second series, too? If your bankroll can handle it, you could raise the bar again, to $10 as your starting bet. Three such sessions will cost over $300, but you have to keep your eye on the statistics. See, if you lose three sessions in a row, you should be due for a serious win streak, since the math calls for you to win 14 of every 15 sessions you play.

But the word from here is: starting out, I advise against any fluctuations in your bets from one session to the next. Then maybe branch out, after you have 50 or 100 sessions under your belt, and you're acclimated to the win rate.

If you *do* try increases after losing sessions, you have to play a very disciplined game. Which means sticking to the procedure, even in the face of disaster. You have to keep the faith that the numbers will (eventually) fall in your favor.

Now, if you're playing online at a casino with $1 minimums, you can cut your costs considerably. An A bet series that shows a profit at all six stages goes $2–$2–$4–$6–$8–$12, and costs $34. The 3Q equivalent is $3–$3–$6–$9–$12–$18.

The key, overall, is to *go for small gains, until your winnings enable you to go for larger gains.* This is a sound approach to any investment scheme, but it is especially important here. If you keep thinking those words with every bet you make—and guide your actions accordingly—you should do all right.

WARNING SIGNS

Fear can take you a long way. Befriend it.

—Kim Basinger
(speaking on the subject of acting)

Under certain circumstances, it might be possible to push the player's edge for the 3Q/A above the 7.22% standard in this book. This goes beyond simply waiting for the right moment to bet; you must also heed the warning signs that the tables are frequently kind enough to provide. There are two:

The first one is when all five of the qualifying numbers are of the same group: A or 3Q. In that case, you would normally bet on the category that hasn't shown up yet, but you might be caught in a weird pattern where the wrong category is going haywire, spitting out nothing but numbers from that group (for the most part). I tend to pass on a table like that.

The second danger sign is when many numbers go by before you get a chance to bet, because non-3Q/A numbers are hitting. The hot tip is no bet, or a small bet. In such cases, I often switch to the T6 (which is covered in Chapter 13) out of sheer boredom, or, out of a sense that I'm wasting my time on something that—after all that waiting—may prove to be a dud.

On the subject of warnings, I must convey the importance of racking up new numbers—one at a time—when playing online at Intercasino or The Sands. Meaning, the five numbers that are on-screen when you enter the game don't accurately reflect the history of that table. More on this in Chapter 13.

FOR THE RECORD

So far, you have seen how the 3Q/A performs when applied against two of the best published system testers now on the market. But there are other statistics to consider, derived from live play. These are not verifiable to the public like the others are, but I'd like to mention them nevertheless, to give you a more rounded view of what to expect.

From *Intercasino,* one of my favorite online casinos, I ended up with an 8.48% statistical advantage over the house, which is not reliable, as the sampling is somewhat limited.

From goldenpalace.com, another online casino (which I *don't* recommend—since they are slow to pay), I ended up with a 9.37% player edge. That high figure may be attributable to the fact that they have single-zero roulette.

Also, I went way back into my files, pulling out a bunch of old scorecards from the Aztar riverboat casino in 1996, and came away with a whopping 13.33% final player edge. Of course, I was not playing the 3Q/A back then, but I was able to use the numbers to theorize what would have been possible.

The upshot of all this is that the 3Q/A works, online and off, with single and double-zero roulette, this year, last year, and years past.

While on the subject of European (single-zero) roulette, it should be noted that the different arrangement of the numbers on the single-zero wheel may impact the effectiveness of the 3Q/A, which was tested primarily against the double-zero wheel. The extent of this impact is still being studied, but in the meantime, players of the 3Q/A are advised to stick to American roulette.

Nothin' but good news.

A WORD ABOUT HEDGING

There are some very knowledgeable people out there who consider me to be something of a fool because I advocate hedging. Well, they're right; I'm a fool. Hedges are stupid. But did you also know that black is white?

And that up is down?

You probably didn't know these things. Lots of things we don't know!

All I can say is, if I'm a fool, I'm damn glad. Because I just love it when a zero comes, and I win. It keeps me in the game for one more spin, which is usually all I need to pull out a win. And when two or three of the green monsters come up in a row, I'm all smiles while everyone else is cursing.

But there's more. Hedging helps me maintain my discipline. It's upsetting to lose that way, and when you're upset you are more likely to stray from the course. And if you stray, well, that's it, so long, good night.

Throughout this chapter, I didn't say a word about hedging for the sake of simplicity. Computing in the hedges tends to make the job messy, and anyway, I can't assume that all my readers are in step with me on this. But if you want to know how I play, I hedge, pal. Every time, when playing the 3Q/A. Just big enough to cover most of my loss, or give me a tiny profit if a zero shows up. I'm not looking to make a big score; I just want some *protection* from the longshot flukes that are out there.

To hedge or not to hedge is up to you, but I do recommend it. After the greenies have burned your butt again and again, I'd think that you're gonna give the matter some thought.

THE ART OF DEALING WITH LOSSES

To win, you have to risk loss.

—Jean-Claude Killy

Nobody likes losses. But when you choose casino gaming as a means of generating income, they are unavoidable. This is one of the inescapable truisms of gaming.

Success in this arena depends almost wholly and completely on how well you deal with losses. If they cause you to lose control, you're finished. Time to go back to the day job.

If you change your perspective, however, they are not so hard to bear. It's all in how you perceive them.

For me, losses are a major part of the natural order of things. I don't mind them, because when I lose a series, I get to regress to a lower betting level. For a brief moment, the pressure is relieved. There's not so much money at stake. Woo hoo!

To be honest, I am not comfortable with the idea of turning over large sums of money. But when I win, the rules call for me to increase the size of my bets. This helps me win more, but I never get used to putting so much money at risk.

Losing is actually something of a comfort, because now I can relax a bit and play for lower stakes. The process becomes a little more mechanical, and it is therefore easier for me to detach myself from the danger that accompanies this existence.

If you think this sounds like crazy talk, then you haven't been properly exposed to the harsh realities of gaming. You are almost certainly playing the denial game.

Don't begrudge your losses. Embrace them.

SUMMARY OF THE 3Q/A

A part of me always believed that a strategy could be devised to overcome the house edge at roulette. But until this book came out, no one had ever done it. Not for lack of trying!

The 3Q/A was an accidental discovery. I had been favoring its two components for many years, but only as part of a freestyle method of play. When I tried merging them to form a two-pronged strategy, it soon became evident that this invention was special, because my win rate improved.

There are three stages of the 3Q/A. First, you have to qualify the table, to determine which of the two components to bet. Then you have to look for the warning signs, as noted on page 144. This is the first stage.

The second stage is the wagering. Each session is comprised of one or two series. When you win one bet, or lose all six from both series, it's time to find another table.

The third stage is when you review the results from the last session, and plot a course for the next. If you're starting out, don't change the wagering structure from one series to the next, because you can put yourself in a big jam in a big hurry if you venture into strange territory too quickly. Wait until you get a hundred or so sessions racked up, and have some familiarity with what to expect, before making the bold moves.

Some readers may wish to make adjustments in the wagering configuration, like going to one three-bet series per session, or two two-bet series. That's okay. But I want to point out that those—and all other feasible variations—have already been tested. What you see here, is what brings in the best numbers.

12

CUSTOMIZED
SCORECARDS

If you have ever played minibaccarat, you may have noticed that most (if not all) players were using a scorecard. That's because the exploitation of patterns is the best way to win at a game that has only two primary betting options. But outside the baccarat pit, the scorecards tend to disappear.

I have always advocated the use of scorecards, for roulette, minibaccarat, and even craps. I believe that one can learn to read the trends of a table, and act upon them with reasonable assurance that doing so will produce results. Of course, any trend could bust the moment you put down your first bet, but if you specialize in certain trends, and act only when the table is putting out the right signals, you'll catch your share of wins.

But it's not just a matter of studying the patterns as you play. While that helps, even more can be gained at the end of the day, when you're evaluating what you did in the comfort of your home. It's important that you keep a record of how you handled yourself in the heat of battle, so you can pinpoint flaws in your technique, and make the necessary adjustments to help ensure that you'll be more prepared next time. This is the best way to avoid repeating your mistakes.

THE ROULETTE SCORECARD

The idea behind the roulette scorecard is to keep the relevant information in full view with every bet. Questions like: how much did I bet six spins back; what's my win and loss ratio; when did the last zero show up; or how much did I win or lose in the last series; can be answered with a quick glance at your scorecard. And since making money in a casino is a serious business, you should avail yourself of all the tools that help make the effort more manageable. This scorecard does the trick.

Let's get right to it. From Figure 33, line 1 is where you enter the name of the casino, which in this case was Argosy. Line 2 is for the session number, and then farther over, the date. Below that is for the time of day, and underneath that, the amount of money IN (before the session), and OUT (after the session).

Lines 3 through 27 are for entering the table data. There is room for five qualifying table results (lines 3 through 7), and then (up to) twenty more results where live betting can be documented. There's a good reason for this design: if you can't make something happen in twenty spins, it's time to move on. The only one likely to benefit from staying longer is the casino.

On to the columns, left to right. Obviously, the first column is for the winning number. Next, R–B–G stands for the color (Red, Black or Green) associated with that number.

The four dashed columns, in order, are for the type of bet; whether that bet won or lost (+ or –); the amount won or lost, and the cumulative monetary standing.

The column of solid lines to the right of the dashed lines is to be used for noting the ebb and flow in your bankroll, if you have the time, and are so inclined.

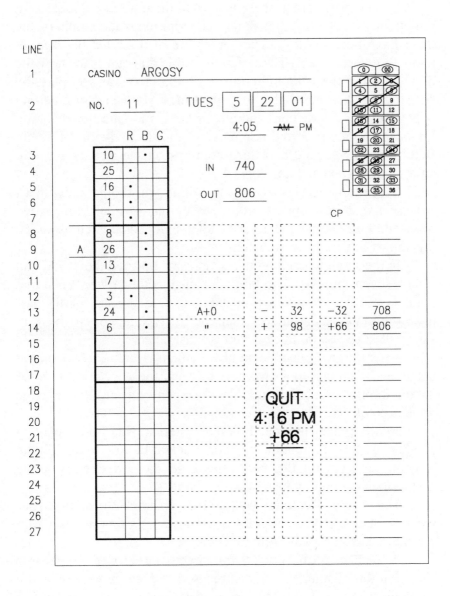

FIGURE 33
The Roulette Scorecard

In the upper corner, there is a small diagram of a double-zero roulette layout. To distinguish the red from the black numbers, the latter have been circled. (The zeroes are also circled, but we all know those are green!) The function of this diagram is to show the distribution of the winning numbers on the layout as you play, by crossing out the ones that won. Sometimes, you can spot a betting opportunity this way. For example, as I was marking this diagram, I noticed that the first four numbers were all from the first column. Betting on the second and third columns on the next spin might have made a good auxiliary bet.

(Regarding that last comment, I think you should know that I *have* seen a 2–1 bet option—like 1st Column—win eight in a row. So, while I might play the described bet under some circumstances, it is not by any means a sure bet.)

In the session noted on this scorecard, I played the 3Q/A, and it took seven spins for A to be established as the target. When that point is reached, a line should be drawn to the left of the last qualifying number (at line 9), then the bet type is written above it. This will keep you on track if you get distracted.

After the first playable number came up (on line 12), I started the series. This one took two bets to catch the win, but I avoided having to play a second series. The "+ 0" entry means that a hedge on the zeroes was added to my A bet.

Auxiliary bets are noted with an asterisk. Had I been playing another strategy, I might have bet on black at line 14, to exploit the (obvious) reoccurring double. In that case, the correct entry in the first dashed column on line 14 would be BLK*.

The + and – column was added separately to clarify your win/loss status. If you see a lot of minuses, it's time to rise from the chair, and step away from the table.

In the back of this book there are templates for the scorecards shown in this chapter, which can be used to print up your own at a copy place like Kinko's. This one was designed to be copied at full scale, "two up" on a letter size sheet of bond, and trimmed just inside the borders. Have them bound into pads of fifty sheets each. You can get several pads for $25 or so.

THE INTERNET SCORECARD

Figure 34 on the following page shows the roulette scorecard as it would look when you cut and paste four copies of Figure 33 onto a sheet of letter-size paper. Then you run copies of the new original, and you'll have the means to chart four sessions on each sheet of paper.

The original configuration was designed that way because, in a casino, table space is frequently limited. There simply isn't room for space-consuming paperwork. And, the smaller size makes it more portable, which can be handy when you're in the habit of moving from table to table.

Playing online, however, is a whole different matter. Usually, space is more abundant (at your home), and the letter-sized sheets are easier to work with and to store.

To answer the question of why the previous scorecards aren't also run four-up: there has to be extra room for trimming when you're dealing with pad binding. Of course, you can try it if you want to save a few quarters, and don't mind that they may end up being out-of-square, but I don't recommend it.

How important is it to record the table and betting activity when playing online? Very important. If something funny happens with your money, that documentation could go a long way toward helping you get things straightened out. Remember, online betting is not a wholly legitimate business at this time (as of this writing). Therefore, the integrity of the transaction is not guaranteed. (More on this subject in the next chapter.)

By the way, Figure 34 shows how the Internet scorecard is to be put together, but this reduced scale image is for viewing only, and is not intended to be copied.

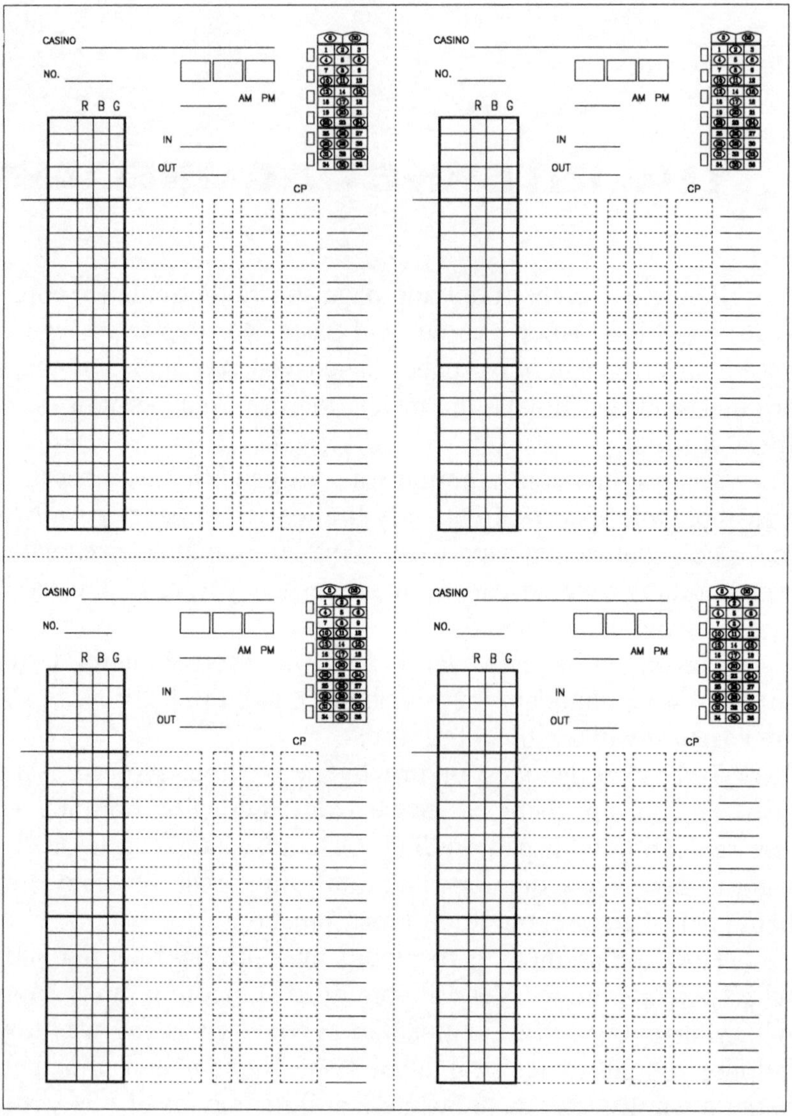

FIGURE 34
*The Internet Scorecard
(Reduced Layout)*

THE STATISTICS SCORECARD

The last scorecard in this series is something I refer to as the statistics scorecard. At the end of the day, end of the trip, or end of the season, this is where you can get an overview of how your bets have performed.

Figure 35 shows the win/loss statistics from a group of 75 sessions of the 3Q/A at Intercasino.com. Since the normal ratio of winning sessions to losing sessions is about 14 to 1, and since I just emerged from a period of winning more than the expected rate, this tells me that I can expect to lose a session in the very near future. Might be a good time to think about going to smaller bets, as a way to protect myself from the inevitable statistical averaging that I would expect to ensue.

There are six rows on this scorecard, each having space for exactly fifty decisions. These could be used to denote the running count of bets, sessions, or anything else that forms some kind of gaming statistic. The W to the left of each row stands for Wins; the L (below that) stands for Losses. Studying table results with odds that match a bet you plan to play can show what kind of winning and losing streaks to anticipate in the future.

I usually use the top two rows for the staples in my wagering diet: 1–1 and/or 2–1 bets. But they're all intended for tracking the bets you customarily play. This scorecard can be used to keep up on how your bets are doing on a given day, or betting activity that spans a period of weeks or even months.

It's nice to have an idea what to expect. That is one more tiny enhancement of the player's edge.

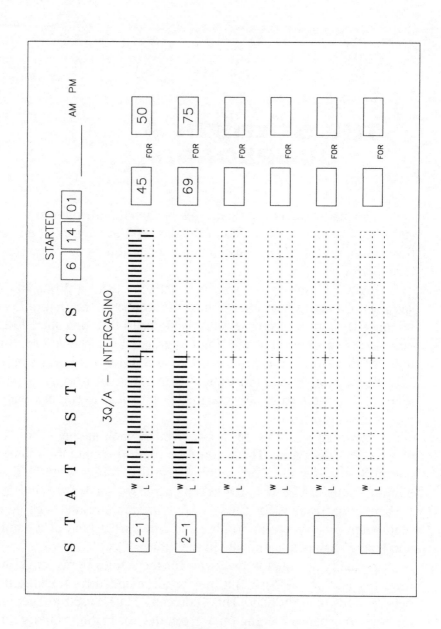

FIGURE 35
The Statistics Scorecard

SUMMARY OF GAMING SCORECARDS

The position of this book is that without scorecards to assist you, you are subjecting yourself to an unnecessary hardship. With them, you can spot trends early, manage your money, and analyze your performance after the fact.

Two scorecards are designed for a finished size of just under 4" by 5½", which is non-intrusive, and yet large enough to hold a generous amount of data. But the one can be restructured so as to be more suitable for online wagering, where it is presumed there is more room than in the limiting confines of a casino.

To recap the scorecard types:

The *roulette scorecard* can help you spot table trends, check your win/loss ratio, and stay on top of every little detail pertaining to the flow of money. You have all the relevant data about what the table *and you* are doing, right at your fingertips.

The *Internet scorecard* gives you four times as much room for table data, because portability and size are not such a concern when you're sitting at your computer.

The *statistics scorecard* gives you a sense of perspective in terms of your collective betting activities. Are you holding your own or underperforming? This can offer valuable insights into the history of your performance.

One last tip: when you get these printed up, you might want to consider having them printed on paper stock in different pastel colors, to help you identify one type from the other. Also, I'm told that doing so may help the ozone layer, since most of the specialty stock contains post-consumer recyclable content.

13

ONLINE WAGERING

It's hard to believe that just a few years ago, what is now a multi-billion dollar business did not even exist. Internet gambling, online wagering and cybercasino gaming are now common phrases used to describe this industry, which is a cultural byproduct of the recent technological advances of mankind. But what is the nature of this beast? Is it a good thing, or a trap?

At the heart of this matter, there reside some rather troubling questions, which should be addressed:

1) Is Internet gambling legal?
2) Are the games honest?
3) Can the operators of those sites be trusted?

These are serious issues: the possibility of having a criminal record, or that your charge card might be billed for unauthorized charges, or that someone might push the *lose* button whenever you take a chance on a large bet.

But lots of people do it every day, right? Doesn't the *safety in numbers* rule apply here? Not necessarily. Even as you read this, the rules are changing at state and federal levels.

THE LEGAL ASPECTS

Before jumping into the online wagering pool with both feet, it might be a good idea to know something about the legal aspects. Meaning, the risk to *you*. We all know that risk is an inherent part of gambling, but we prefer to think that the risk is controlled. We don't need to compound it with a possibility of criminal penalties, or financial debt that we did not incur.

To lend insight into this complicated issue, the following is a brief history of what the government is trying to do, and why the matter is so difficult to resolve.

In 1995, when online gaming was in its infancy, Senator Jon Kyl of Arizona introduced an amendment to the Crime Prevention Act of 1995, known as the Internet Gambling Prohibition Act. It was passed by the U.S. Senate, but couldn't get through the House of Representatives. In the years that followed, it was reintroduced with significant amendments, but it has never made it through both houses of Congress, as of the date of this writing.

The original bill contained a provision that made it a federal misdemeanor to place a bet on the Internet, but that effort has since been abandoned. So, why is it so hard for Congress to pass a law to restrict Internet gaming? There are some good reasons.

One of these is revealed in the question: how can the U.S. or any state government impose its authority on a transaction that originated from outside its borders—without impinging on the sovereignty of a foreign government? All online casinos are based outside the U.S., in places like the Caribbean, Europe, and Africa. And the associated governments aren't overly concerned about a business that brings wealth into their country.

Some governments, in fact, operate the games themselves! Liechtenstein will accept bets from anywhere in the world, except for its two neighbors, Austria and Switzerland.

The problem is this: since websites are passive, and the user receives the signal electronically, there is no way to stop it at the border. Also, international law does not allow for someone from one country to arrest a citizen of another country, who may in fact be licensed by his own government.

Even if this issue didn't center around the personal computer, I understand there's a website, MonaCall, which offers cybercasino gambling from a touch-tone phone!

What about the ISPs? Can't America Online, for instance, be held accountable? Nope. Under current law, telephone companies and Internet service providers are not criminally liable if, say, an illegal bookie uses a telephone line. And, you can bet that there would be enormous public outcry if the utility companies started monitoring the habits of their customers.

What's left? Prosecuting the bettors? That won't work. The U.S. Department of Justice doesn't have the manpower to enforce another set of laws that would criminalize a whole new segment of the population. Nor do they want to be in the business of arresting casual gamblers.

But that doesn't stop the states from passing their own laws. As of July 2001, quite a few states have either passed laws or have legislation pending that would make it a crime to accept a bet over the Internet.

And, as if things weren't confusing enough already, in April 2001, the state of Nevada passed a bill that legalizes online gaming in that state. But subsequently, I learned that the Nevada Gaming Commission was hiring an East Coast law firm to see if what they plan to do is allowable under federal law!

For the time being, it appears that both the player and house sides of this issue can operate with some measure of impunity, but that probably won't last forever. If online wagering appeals to you, it is the recommendation of this book that you first check out the laws within your state of residence.

ASSESSING THE DOMAIN

As of August 2001, there were more than 900 online gaming establishments operating in over thirty countries. Most of these sites are regulated in some way, but quite a few of them are not accountable to any agency or government. Obviously, the ones that aren't regulated are the ones to avoid. But even if one locates, and then eliminates the baddies, how can a suitable online casino be chosen from the hundreds that remain? And once a choice is made, how does one intelligently assess that domain?

Since the U.S. government has no authority over operations that are based outside its borders, the industry has been making the effort to regulate itself. The following are a few of these agencies, listed in order according to the author's preference:

 The *Internet Gaming Commission* seems to have the most comprehensive database of all those I've visited, and the fact that they won't accept banner advertising is evidence of their integrity. The web address is www.internetcommission.com.

The *Ethical Online Business Association* may be the second best source for information about web casinos.

The *Interactive Gaming Council* was at one time one of the leaders in its category, but their database of recommended casinos isn't as vast or well-organized as "the other IGC."

The *Antigua-Barbuda Directorate of Offshore Licensing* also was prominent in its day, but I can no longer find them.

Safebet appears to be an industry shill, which gives bad leads.

So, out of the five that I believed to be the most prominent a year or two ago, only the first two seem to be properly maintained. I wanted to make a point of noting this, because this corrects what I said about these sites in my last book, and it shows how quickly things can change with web-based ventures.

If you're planning to do some online wagering, I recommend that you pay a visit to the Internet Gaming Commission website. But for the record, here's the quick tour:

On the home page, there are some browser buttons to the left. Click on *Directories,* and you will see:

- Licensed & Accredited Gaming Sites (28 as of Mar. 2002)
- Licensed Gaming Sites (453 as of March 2002)
- Licensed, Audit in Process (159 as of March 2002)
- Licensed, Information Incomplete (107 as of Mar. 2002)
- Licensed, Caution Urged (47 as of March 2002)
- Extreme Caution Urged (56 as of March 2002)
- Unlicensed Gaming Sites (125 as of March 2002)

These are hyperlinks, which will take you to the lists for each category. The top category, *Licensed & Accredited Gaming Sites,* refers to casinos that are not only licensed, but also submitted to an accreditation process. These supposedly offer the highest level of customer service and satisfaction, by:

- Ensuring prompt responses to dispute resolution inquiries
- Guaranteeing customer privacy and confidentiality
- Ensuring that all advertising is truthful
- Prohibiting minors from accessing their gaming systems
- Paying all winnings and account balances on demand
- Maintaining an audit trail for all customers

These points form a powerful argument, but don't read too much into this. Many casinos from the second category do all of the above, but haven't yet submitted to accreditation.

For the record, www.goldenpalace.com, which I referred to on page 145 as one that I don't recommend, is at this writing in the *Extreme Caution Urged* category. My complaint with them is that they are quick to take your money, but slow to pay winnings. If not for having some pull as a gaming writer, I'm not sure I would have gotten my winnings when I did.

The IGC website had this to say about Golden Palace:

We have received numerous complaints about this site and its affiliate site, Casino Depot, cancelling winnings from customers under its complaint of Promotion Abuse. It appears that they offer these promotions and cancel if the customer wins.

So, how did I end up playing at this website? They have been running ads in a gaming magazine, and I believed that magazine would not endorse—through permission to advertise—anything less than a reputable establishment. What this shows, is that one has to be wary of false illusions that can be presented to the public. I should have taken the advice I now offer, and checked them out first at the IGC site.

Ahead in this chapter, I have something to say about a family of online casinos that gave me even bigger headaches, and how to deal with that situation.

But you need to find one that *won't* be a source of problems. My favorites are *Intercasino* and *Sands of the Caribbean,* because unlike most sites, you don't have to have a bet riding every spin. This gives you the chance to wait for the right table signs before placing a bet. You might want to start with the *Sands,* because they have single-zero roulette and $1 minimums, whereas *Intercasino* has double-zero games and $5 minimums. Both sites are licensed with the Internet Gaming Commission.

In seeking a suitable online casino, one of the considerations is which of the three types you prefer. The first type requires you to download the program, which takes time. The software is free, but it will be stored on your hard drive. The two casinos mentioned in the previous paragraph are from this category.

The second type uses JAVA applets, which run through your browser (instead of a downloaded program). Some, but not all, of these casinos offer both sound and animation.

The third type uses all HTML and does not require download time. They are not as sophisticated as the other types, but do have good graphics and fast gameplay.

But if you are new to the business of online wagering, these are minor issues. What you really want is some assurance that your money will be safe, and the games are honest.

Here's a few things you should know:

1) All of the reputable Internet casinos use a random number generator to produce their gaming results, which is an integral part of the program sold to them by the software manufacturer. These programs are encrypted by the software company, locking out the casino's ability to modify the programming.

2) These software programs record all the bets and results, and the time they occurred. Everything you did while wagering online can be reconstructed.

3) Most online casinos don't get your credit card number. The monetary transfer is handled by a third-party processor, who then forwards the money—minus your credit card number—to the casino. Doing it this way is how the casino gets around the Travel Act, which would permit the U.S. government to claim jurisdiction over monetary transfers directly from player to casino.

4) If you see the seal of the Internet Gaming Commission or the Ethical Online Gaming Association at the website, the casino in question should be okay.

5) Another positive sign is if the casino has good phone or email support when needed.

6) Some e-casinos and many of the software developers are publicly traded companies, which means that their books are open to the world. They wouldn't stay in business long if they engaged in unethical business practices.

Then there's something else to consider: at a larger site, do you think the casino has the manpower to monitor all the games in progress at any given point in time?

We're talking about a company hiring hundreds or thousands of people to sit there and doctor up the table results, and keep it a secret from the world, forever? Trying to meet the payroll for that would be much more expensive than to just let the games grind out the profit that comes automatically!

Now, if you put together all the pieces I've just described, it should be evident that there is some measure of safety in the realm of online wagering. This comes from the fact that the components are separated: the casino doesn't get your credit card number, and it is also powerless to modify the encrypted gaming program. But we're talking reputable casinos. If they haven't been licensed by the IGC, these layers of security could devolve to a fine powder, not unlike that which is used as a pigment for cheap cosmetics, and that could spell trouble with a capital T.

But you still have one nagging concern, which I also share: would it not be possible for some casinos to fool the regulatory agency into thinking that its operations are legitimate, when it does in fact have the means to control the programming whenever the player puts down a large bet?

Even I cannot offer an assurance against this possibility, but there is a way to protect yourself in such a case: start out betting small, and notate all the table decisions. As your bankroll grows, you can bet larger from the money you won. That way, any loss you sustain will involve mostly *won money.*

To add yet another level of security, you can do a study of the table results after you've racked up several thousand spins of play. If the numbers aren't coming up in line with the probabilities, it'll show up. Then, you'll have documentation to support any case you wish to pursue against the casino.

But the key question to ask is: *are you winning?* If you have been sticking to the rules but you can't seem to win, this is a sign that something might not be right.

The final criterion for assessing the domain is to make sure the casino has what are called *multi-player games.* This means that the program won't shut down if you fail to place a bet. And that's a feature that shouldn't be overlooked.

TRACKING YOUR BETS

As noted on the previous page, charting the table decisions when playing online is a form of insurance against the possibility that the casino you've chosen is not wholly legit. You never really know what's behind table results that are technically a cartoon, as is the case with online casinos. So, it would be wise to have some documentation to support your position. The Internet scorecard, as discussed in the last chapter, is ideal for this.

But how does one authenticate a set of random table results? According to Erick St. Germain's *Roulette System Tester,* the least occurences of any number, from any set of 1000 numbers, was 16. The most was 50. These figures represent the highs and lows of the statistical variance in any group of 1000 spins, from a sampling of 15,000. Statistically, every number should come up 26.32 times out of every 1000 spins at American roulette, but that's an average. What I'm saying is that if you count the times any number wins from a group of 1000 spins, and find that some are coming up less than 16 or more than 50 times, this could be a red flag.

This range is not absolute, but it does serve as an indicator of a reasonable probabilistic expectation.

By the way, the *Roulette System Tester* mentioned above is published by the Zumma Publishing Company, Arlington, Texas, and is available at the *Gambler's Book Shop* in Las Vegas, which can be reached at 1-800-522-1777.

But there is another, larger purpose for tracking your wagers. You need to see the history of your performance, so you can see if you've been sticking to the game plan. In effect, this helps keep you honest, *with yourself.*

ONLINE STRATEGIES

Before the existence of online wagering, anyone seeking to make it as a serious player had a hard way to go. He would have to save up enough to cover the cost of a large bankroll, travel costs, and living expenses to carry him until he could support himself with his new vocation. This also involved negotiating time off with his employer, or quitting his job, which frequently meant burning some bridges. This is not exactly a confidence-builder at a time when one tends to feel most vulnerable to the harsh realities of life. Therefore, few of those who tried had even the slimmest chance of success in that endeavor.

Online wagering changed that overnight. With an investment of just a few hundred dollars, anyone of legal age, armed with a sound strategy, can begin the process of building a bankroll in his spare time, while seated comfortably at his desk. What was once virtually unattainable is no longer so.

One of the advantages of online wagering is the absence of the *disadvantages* of the alternative:

When you walk into a land casino, you're on their turf. You are in an environment that was specifically designed to make you lose control. You're inundated by the sensations they've created to trigger your compulsive nature.

Maybe you can rise above all that, but the casinos don't make it easy. You're a fat pigeon on the hot pavement.

Then there's the time spent traveling to the casino, money for gas, meals, and expenses. It all adds up.

If you want to make money, betting online is the path of least resistance. For *my* money, that's the high road.

TARGETED SIXLINES (T6)

In all the figures of roulette scorecards in this book, you may have noticed six small rectangular boxes to the left of the roulette diagram. These are for noting the distribution of winning numbers on a roulette layout. The point of this feature is to help you identify a wagering opportunity.

At most roulette tables, the numbers fill out the layout pretty fast. From any point in time, it is unlikely that the next six winners will come from a concentrated section of the layout, which means that the *rest* of the layout is fair game.

To assist in capitalizing on this, I have divided the layout into six groups of sixlines, starting with the numbers 1–6, and moving upward from there. Thus, the top box applies to numbers from the 1–6 group; next is 7–12; then 13–18, etc. Of course, there are other ways to form sixlines (e.g., 4–9 or 16–21), but this configuration was chosen for simplicity.

Figure 36 shows a scorecard of mine from a session I played online at the *Sands of the Caribbean*. Bearing in mind the fact that the numbers that are showing when entering an online game can't be trusted, I generated a new set. From that set, the first five spins produced winners from four sixlines, which shows how quickly the numbers can spread across the layout. When they spread that fast, the odds are good that trend will continue.

How does one capitalize on this? There are quite a few ways, but I prefer to target the neglected areas, from a recent set of table decisions. Starting from a blank slate, I wait until winning numbers have landed in four of the sixlines. Then I target the remaining two sixlines, which form a bet that pays 2–1.

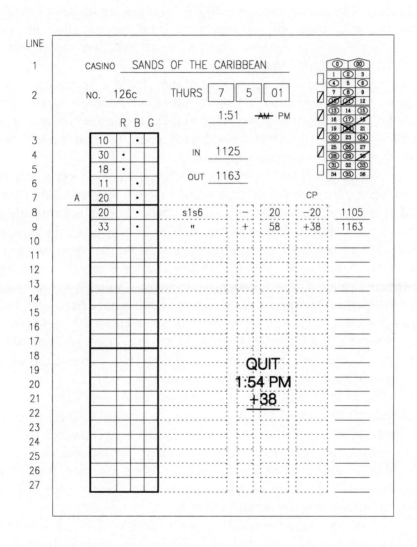

FIGURE 36
A Targeted Sixline Scorecard

Some players might favor waiting for three sixlines to hit, then playing the remaining three for a 1–1 return. That, too, can be effective. Or, you could wait until *four* sixlines are hit, then bet the two neglected ones plus the last one that hit, as protection against repeating numbers. As you can see, doing that here would have caught a 1–1 winner on the first bet.

Whatever you decide, the important thing is to wait for the optimum table condition: a pattern where the numbers spread out quickly, from the time you start the clock. If you see the numbers getting hung up in certain areas, this is your clue that the table is not suited for this wagering approach.

Now, if I had been playing the 3Q/A, the correct move would have been to first establish the wagering target, which would be the A bet in this example. In that case, the procedure calls for waiting for an A number to pop up before betting. It was just coincidence that the two neglected sixlines happened to be the same two that form the A bet, so I ended up chasing the same target—but with different timing. The A number that came up on line 9 was the win for the sixline strategy, but that same number would have been the trigger for the A side of the 3Q/A. I'll never know if I could have also caught a 3Q/A winner, because all I was seeking was one win, and got it after just three minutes of play. That's one of the nice features of surgical strikes online: fast results.

So, what kind of series is recommended for this? That mostly depends on the payoff you're pursuing (1–1 or 2–1). Don't exceed a three-bet series, unless you want to wait for *five* sixlines to hit, then pursue the 5–1 return on the remaining sixline. For that, you could go to more stages, since it's more like a longshot. But for a 1–1 return, I would say no more than two bets, and for the 2–1, a two- or three-bet series should be the limit.

At tables where the numbers don't spread quickly, you might want to improvise on the strategy, and target the three sixlines that have already hit, for a 1–1 return. If you lose to a non-zero, add the newest sixline, and drop the one that was the first to hit, from the group you last covered. This technique works well at tables with repeating numbers, which are very common.

FREESTYLE WAGERING

There is another way to play surgical strikes which has not yet been mentioned in this book. It involves a similar approach, but with smaller, more varied bets, and more of them. The term I use for this is *freestyle wagering.*

This is hard to convey, because it simultaneously involves less risk, and more risk. The *less risk* aspect comes from spreading the risk across a greater number of bets. The *more risk* derives from having to be completely *on your toes* every second of the session. That being the case, I would tend to assume that many of my readers couldn't handle the demands of this wagering format, because of the level of stress involved. And yes, be forewarned; playing this way is very stressful.

So, it is with some hesitation that I show this to you, but it's the way I play, and it has been very effective for me. And I would have paid dearly to have had someone to teach it to me many years ago, for it would have helped me immeasurably. Just don't forget my warning: if you try this, go slow, and expect setbacks. If you're not winning, dump it. Do something else.

Freestyle wagering, as described herein, involves a mentality of looking for chinks in the armor of your opponent. With every move the table makes, you're looking to find a tiny vulnerability, a weakness of some kind, just big enough to give you an opening to gain even the slightest advantage. Then you keep circling, dancing, thrusting and jabbing. One by one, all these little pinpricks will add up to your victory, and his defeat.

As an abstract concept, this all sounds great, doesn't it? But how is it carried out in real life?

To accomplish this, I need to show you the stages of gaming activity from a recent scorecard of mine. For the record, the next nine figures show a representation of that scorecard, which has been altered to highlight the key data elements. Figure 46, at the end of that run, shows a more accurate depiction of the scorecard as it appeared when the session ended.

Figure 37—the first of these figures—shows the beginning of a session I played at Intercasino.com. The following (eight) figures show the gaming activity, spin by spin. Now remember, the spins that are on screen when you "arrive" at the casino are not authentic table results. The only numbers that are valid are those you witness as you play. I learned this from jumping out and then back into the game on a number of occasions.

After generating five new numbers (with the *pass* button), I didn't initially see any solid bets. But as the spin was in progress, I noticed that all of the last five spins landed in the second column, and was lamenting the fact that I missed the play on columns one and three. But mercifully, the next spin also landed in column two! A mishap turns into a blessing.

But there's another factor in play. I usually keep one eye on the 3Q/A whenever I play, and that sixth spin was also my cue to make an A bet. Which bet should get priority? I decided that the columns bet was a surer thing, so I put a quarter on each column, then added $5 on each of the "A" sixlines, and a $3 hedge on the zeroes. The hedge was to small to be anything more than a token bet, but that's usually how I do it when I'm pursuing more than one wagering target.

Up pops a 12, an A loser, but a columns bet winner. That's okay. I still have two more chances to hit the A before the series is exhausted.

Figure 38 shows the result of my first bet, and what I chose as my follow-up bet. Since I was now going after only one target (disregarding the hedge), I pressed my A bet up to $10 on each of the sixlines, and put $2 on the 0-00.

Figure 39 shows the result of my second bet. After that, I sat out the next table decision (shown as *no bet*).

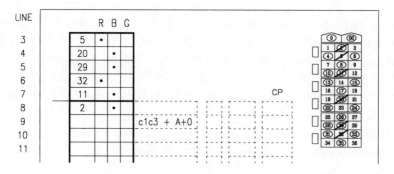

FIGURE 37
Freestyle Scorecard, View 1

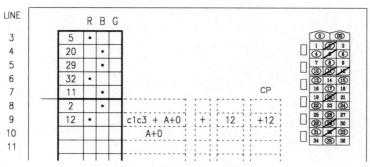

FIGURE 38
Freestyle Scorecard, View 2

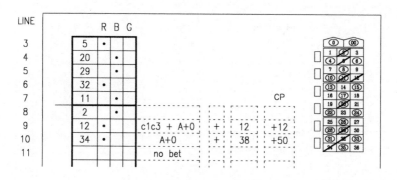

FIGURE 39
Freestyle Scorecard, View 3

Not playing that spin turned out to be a lucky move, because that gave me time to look things over, and make the observation that the table was showing a pattern of alternating sledgehammers. When 16 came up on the non-played spin, I realized that that if I had been alternating between the two sledges, I would have won the last seven spins. Definitely worth a shot. At that point, the table was primed for a win from group B, so (on line 12) I put a $60 bet on the sledge B and added a $2 zeroes hedge.

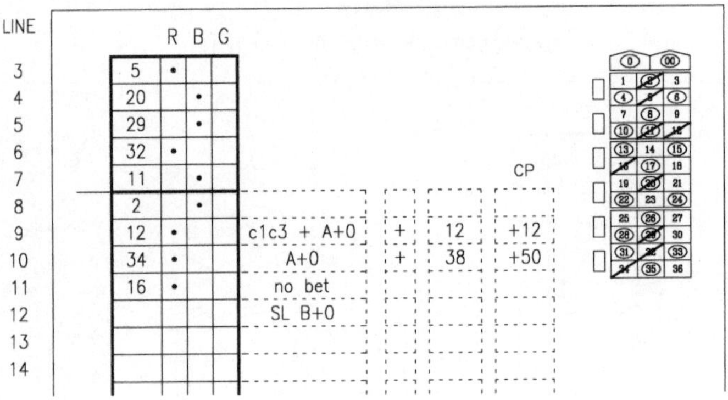

FIGURE 40
Freestyle Scorecard, View 4

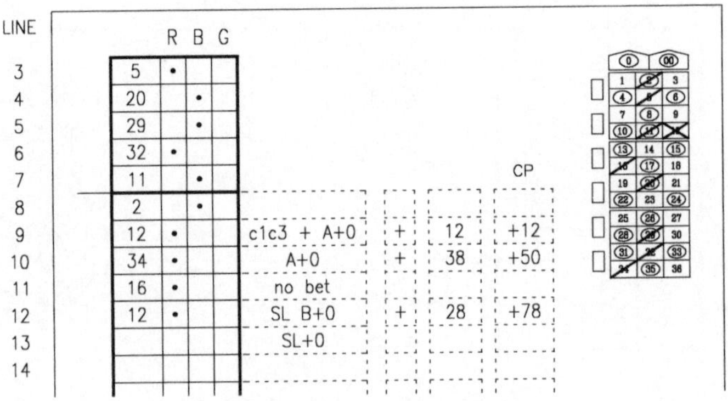

FIGURE 41
Freestyle Scorecard, View 5

My $62 bet produced a $28 win. Was it worth it? Sure.

For the next spin, the sledge A had come into rotation, but it was time to regress, so I played $40 plus a $2 hedge. The 15 won, giving me a profit of $18 (see Figure 42).

The follow-up was sledge B, which I played as outside bets (1st and 3rd 12s), skipping the hedge. That returned an even $20. After that, it's back to the sledge A (see Figure 43).

LINE		R	B	G								
3	5	•									
4	20		•								
5	29		•								
6	32	•									
7	11		•					CP			
8	2		•								
9	12	•			c1c3 + A+0	+	12	+12			
10	34	•			A+0	+	38	+50			
11	16	•			no bet						
12	12	•			SL B+0	+	28	+78			
13	15		•		SL+0	+	18	+96			
14					SL B						
15											

FIGURE 42
Freestyle Scorecard, View 6

LINE		R	B	G								
3	5	•									
4	20		•								
5	29		•								
6	32	•									
7	11		•					CP			
8	2		•								
9	12	•			c1c3 + A+0	+	12	+12			
10	34	•			A+0	+	38	+50			
11	16	•			no bet						
12	12	•			SL B+0	+	28	+78			
13	15		•		SL+0	+	18	+96			
14	11		•		SL B	+	20	+116			
15					SL+0						

FIGURE 43
Freestyle Scorecard, View 7

It wasn't too much of a shock when the trend tanked on the next spin, since I had already regressed once again. What caused the loss, though, was an angel number, so I opted to launch one last series, on the angel (Figure 44). The first bet lost, so I repeated the bet, increasing slightly (Figure 45).

LINE		R	B	G					
3	5	•							
4	20		•						
5	29		•						
6	32	•							
7	11		•					CP	
8	2		•						
9	12	•		c1c3 + A+0	+	12	+12	
10	34	•		A+0	+	38	+50	
11	16	•		no bet				
12	12	•		SL B+0	+	28	+78	
13	15		•	SL+0	+	18	+96	
14	11		•	SL B	+	20	+116	
15	5	•		SL+0	−	21	+95	
16				A+0				

FIGURE 44
Freestyle Scorecard, View 8

LINE		R	B	G					
3	5	•							
4	20		•						
5	29		•						
6	32	•							
7	11		•					CP	
8	2		•						
9	12	•		c1c3 + A+0	+	12	+12	
10	34	•		A+0	+	38	+50	
11	16	•		no bet				
12	12	•		SL B+0	+	28	+78	
13	15		•	SL+0	+	18	+96	
14	11		•	SL B	+	20	+116	
15	5	•		SL+0	−	21	+95	
16	28		•	A+0	−	20	+75	
17				"				

FIGURE 45
Freestyle Scorecard, View 9

Just when I was starting to question the wisdom of launching a series that put my gains at risk at the end of a session, my $30 bet on the angel wins, netting me $58 after deducting for the $2 hedge. I end the session with a gain of $133 (Figure 46).

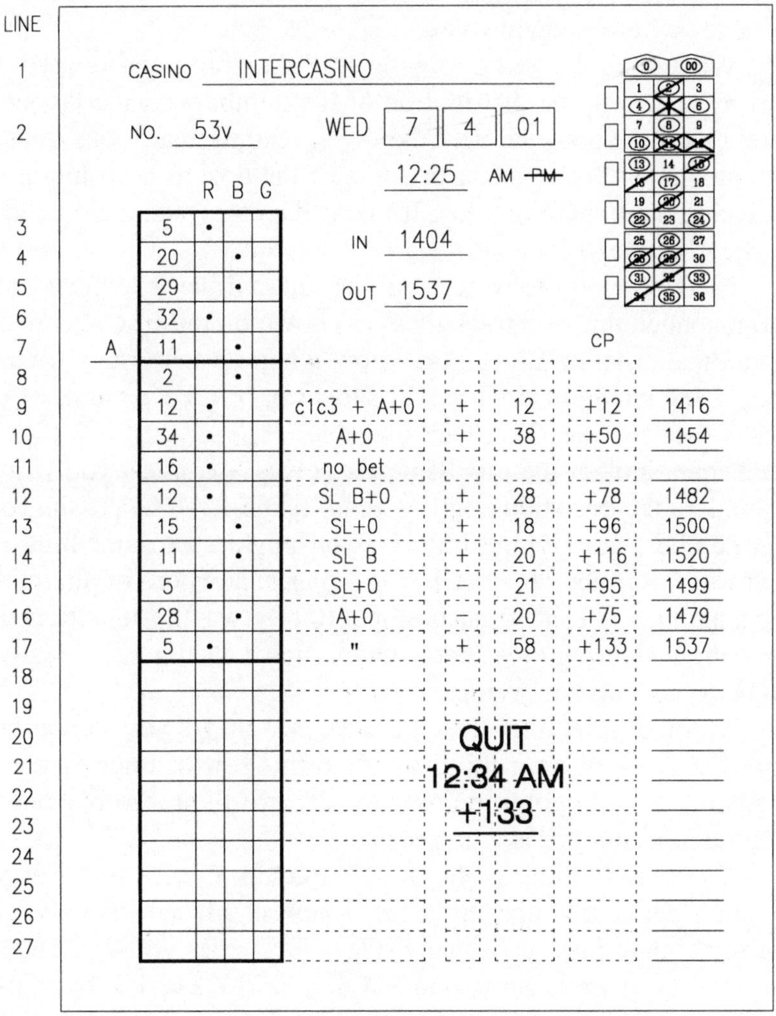

LINE		R B G					
1	CASINO	INTERCASINO					
2	NO. 53v	WED 7 4 01					
		12:25 AM ~~PM~~					
3	5 •	IN 1404					
4	20 •						
5	29 •	OUT 1537					
6	32 •						
7	A 11 •	CP					
8	2 •						
9	12 •	c1c3 + A+0	+	12	+12	1416	
10	34 •	A+0	+	38	+50	1454	
11	16 •	no bet					
12	12 •	SL B+0	+	28	+78	1482	
13	15 •	SL+0	+	18	+96	1500	
14	11 •	SL B	+	20	+116	1520	
15	5 •	SL+0	−	21	+95	1499	
16	28 •	A+0	−	20	+75	1479	
17	5 •	"	+	58	+133	1537	
18							

QUIT
12:34 AM
+133

FIGURE 46
Freestyle Scorecard, View 10

Now, one thing you should know about playing this way is that it's very demanding. So, please, don't be looking at the rate of return ($133 in 9 minutes), and try to work it out to an hourly rate. That would be a mistake. It doesn't work that way. You have to be totally psyched for each session. If you play too long or too often, the tables will turn against you.

What should you be looking for? Anything and everything. Start by checking the distribution of the numbers on the layout. Is there anything about the way they're spreading that looks unusual or exploitable? Perhaps one or some of the dozens or columns are not seeing their share of wins. If this is the case, take a closer look. Maybe it's time to try a brief series.

Next, look at the patterns in the red and black numbers. It is recommended that you track them as shown on these scorecards, as an automatic habit. You never know when an extremely obvious reoccurring single or double will show up, or a P3 pattern, or one of the other patterns. These are playable.

Then, look at the numbers themselves. At times, you will hit a table like the one shown in Figure 24 (page 121), where the fixed split numbers are kicking butt. Or you might spot something like what was described on these last few pages: a pattern of alternating sledgehammers. That wagering opportunity was not mentioned in the section covering those bets, which shows what a little creativity can do to widen your options.

If you decide to try this, there are two things you should keep at the forefront of your thinking: first, this sort of thing is not for sluggards. You've got to be on the ball. Exit the cargo bay and hit the ground running. Take no prisoners.

The second thing is the most important of all: whatever you do, don't get caught chasing a bet. Know in advance exactly what you're going to play, how many stages of a series you'll allow, and how much you are willing to invest. If you lose a series, back away from it and look for something else. Don't change the plan in the middle of the game, and be prepared to write off losses from a ploy that didn't work.

Circle and pounce, then retreat. That's the game.

THE PROS AND CONS
OF ONLINE WAGERING

What are the good and the bad points about online wagering? Here's one point of view.
The pros:

1) Travel expenses to and from casinos are eliminated. This includes gas, meals, vehicle maintenance, and sometimes, admission.
2) It saves time. You don't have spend hours in transit.
3) Admission is always free.
4) Most online casinos offer (ongoing) matchplay bonuses with your deposits. Free money!
5) There is little or no pressure to bet. You can wait all day for the right table condition.
6) You don't have to suffer the sounds and sensations land casinos use to trigger your compulsive nature.
7) You don't have to fight the crowds.
8) You don't have to deal with high table minimums.
9) Because of their low overhead, e-casinos can offer better games (like European roulette).
10) Many virtual casinos have practice modes, where you can test your playing skill, for free. Some sites offer nothing *but* practice games.
11) Playing while seated at a desk in your own home is more convenient and comfortable.
12) At home, you don't have to worry about pickpockets and rail thieves.

And now, the cons:

1) The accessibility of online casinos can become a liability for those who can't handle the seductiveness of gaming. *Click a mouse, lose a house* is not widely regarded as a happy thought.
2) Use of a credit card (for the buy-in and deposits) tends to keep the player detached from the ultimate cost. This can compound the damage noted in item 1.
3) In trying to qualify for a match-play bonus, some players may stay at the tables longer than intended, causing them to lose more than intended.
4) Some online casinos are dishonest. They are a vanishing breed, but you can't assume that all online casinos are as legit as their land-based counterparts.
5) Online gaming may actually be illegal in your state. The penalties are not severe, but you are advised to look into the matter before getting in too deep.
6) Online casinos can't duplicate the sensations and genuine feel of a land casino, if that's what you seek.
7) The decision to play online is more complex. You have to deal with reading lists like this one!

Do not be misled by the greater quantity of pros than cons. The negatives can carry more weight, because we're talking about the possibility of people's lives being ruined.

Some people may take comfort in knowing that large credit card debts to online casinos—when challenged by the person who racked up the bills—are frequently adjudged to be uncollectable. Meaning, the bank usually sides with the gambler (its customer) over what is often presumed to be a sleazy offshore operation. But the circumstances and laws surrounding web-related issues have a way of changing overnight. For that reason (among others), relying on this as a bail-out is a really *bad* idea!

Obviously, online wagering has its good and bad points. Best thing to do is to keep your eyes open.

WHAT TO DO IF YOU'VE BEEN FLIM-FLAMMED

In matters of style, swim with the current; in matters of principle, stand like a rock.

—Thomas Jefferson

If you plan to play online, you cannot unconditionally rule out the possibility that you'll be flim-flammed by the casino. Just because it looks big, and/or was recommended by a rating service, is not a guarantee of ethical business conduct.

Does everybody out there know what *flim-flammed* means? What I'm talking about is web casinos taking your money, either by reneging on a promised bonus, or stalling when you would like to cash out, or outright theft of your credit card funds. And since this may be out of the jurisdiction of the U.S. government, this is a topic which should not be ignored.

To help you see the nature of the problem, a brief history of my adverse experiences might be of some use. Back on page 163, I said that www.goldenpalace.com was a site that was *slow to pay.* But there's more to it than just a lack of speed.

When I tried to cash out at Golden Palace, I was informed that a bank wire will take 5 to 7 business days, and cost $15. What they don't tell you is that *your* bank will probably charge another $15 (or so) at the receiving end.

If you want your check sent by registered mail, that costs $10 per $1000, and takes 2 to 6 weeks to arrive.

The quickest way to get your money is usually with Fed Ex, but that takes 5 to 7 business days, and costs $35.

What's happening here is that you're being penalized for the fact that they're located offshore, in a location where mail costs are high, and the service is slow.

Ah, but it doesn't end there. It isn't until you try to withdraw your funds that they tell you that:

Please note that it takes 5 to 7 business days for us to process your disbursement request (after you have sent the email) prior to the time that your winnings are sent.

Jeez Louise! What this means, is that the economical choice could take up to eight weeks, and the quickest (but expensive) way will probably take about three weeks.

Now, remember: web casinos don't have the huge operating costs of the land counterparts, so they should be swimming in cash. Therefore, if they aren't *Johnny-on-the-spot* when it's time to cash out, this strikes me as a glaring red flag. As you may well imagine, I never went back to Golden Palace.

How did they get my business? I first became aware of them through an ad in a well-known gaming magazine, in which they referred to themselves as *the most popular gaming site on the Net*. That was the hook, but what reeled me in was the lure of deposit bonuses of 100%, up to a certain amount.

But as you read earlier in this chapter, the Internet Gaming Commission said that it *appears* that they cancel the bonus if you happen to win. (I didn't know that at the time.)

The message is: beware of the casinos promising a big bonus, for you may never actually see the money. In fairness, I should mention that Golden Palace did come through in the end (for me), but the whole thing left a bad taste in my mouth.

That encounter, however, is not nearly the headache I had to endure at another gaming site. So, let us now turn to the subject of a family of five online casinos:

- www.americasonlinecasino.com
- www.clubregalcasino.com
- www.clubmardigrascasino.com
- www.eworldcasino.com
- www.cleopatrascasino.com

These casinos came to my attention—one at a time—through a series of newsletters that somehow ended up in my email inbox. These newsletters present themselves as unbiased news reports on where the best deals are for online casino bonuses, etc. This false impression is validated by the fact that week after week, different casinos are mentioned. Ultimately, I came to realize, however, that this is nothing more than the self-promotion of five online casinos that are owned by the same company.

But the bonuses were hard to resist. And during a period in which I lost $100, they paid the bonus. But only in cyberspace, and only when I lost. When I won and tried to cash out, things had a way of getting difficult.

Before that point was reached, however, there were red flags I should have acknowledged. The first was when—after loading the software—it came to my attention that the table minimums were higher than I expected. I called customer service, and the guy directed me to another one of their casinos. When I asked about crediting the funds (from the wrong casino) back to my charge card, he said that he could make the transfer to the other casino. This was a surprise, for I thought all online casinos used a third-party processor for the transaction, and therefore do not know your credit card number. When I asked him how he was able to access my number, he said: *"I'm looking right at it."*

Uh-oh. Sleaze alert. This is not a good sign, for two reasons: first, the most important layer of security, third-party transfer of funds, did not exist. Second, if the money is transferred directly from player to casino, the U.S. government can assume jurisdiction over the matter, under the Travel Act. And that means both sides could be subject to penalties.

So, how did I handle this? I made a mental note, then forgot about it. See, I was in the hunt for that big bonus.

That was the first red flag. The second one involved table results that were highly suspect. During a brief wagering period, number 17 won four out of six spins. That in itself is not unusual. But it so happens that those four bets, and only those four, were about 30 times the size of all my other bets!

In other words, at the precise moment I pressed my bets up to the skies, the number 17, a loser, was right there. For all of my bets (and only those bets) that involved large sums.

Now, this could all be coincidence. I cannot make a rational claim that those decisions were fixed, because like I say, anything can happen at the tables.

But, I have to say, it smells bad.

A short time later, I put two and two together, and decided it was time to stop playing at that casino. I went to the online cashier to cash out the $90 remaining in my account. After that, I emailed their customer support, asking them to confirm the time, date, and amount of the transfer.

They replied, showing the correct figures for the request. But there was no indication that the request was approved, which has to happen for the money to move.

A few days later, I sent a new email, asking when the money was, or would be, credited back to my card. Their reply:

Regarding your query, the $90 you are referring to is pending to go back to your credit card.

It will be approved tomorrow. Once we do it, we will send you a verification email.

At that point, one week had elapsed since I made the request. I waited a few days—during which time I assumed the matter was taken care of—before writing to ask if the money was credited to my card on schedule. The reply:

Thak you (sic) for choosing us at ClubMardiGras Casino!!!! We're glad to have you here with us!!!

Regarding your query, the reason for the delay is that we're having problems with our bank. This conflict is going to be solved soon, cause we're planning to change banks.

At this point, I was starting to lose hope, and, prepare myself for the possibility of losing the money. But, I decided to wait four more days, then write them again:

"How are you coming with the $90 withdrawal I requested on March 29? Do I assume correctly that it will be taken care of soon? If not, I'll need a specific estimate from you."

Regarding your query, we have already approved your payout for the $90. We are really sorry for the delay. You should see it on your statement in 7 to 10 days.

But this turned out to be untrue. I wrangled with them for two more weeks, then decided it was time to take stronger measures. So I sent emails to the customer support links for all five casinos, detailing the problem and saying that if the matter was not remedied immediately, I would take the following action:

1) A formal complaint will be filed with the Internet Gaming Commission, the Interactive Gaming Council, and the Ethical Online Gaming Association.

2) An article, detailing the problem, will be submitted to rgtgaming.com online magazine, naming the five casinos.

3) A similar article will be sent to Casino Player magazine.

4) A detailed description of the problem will be posted on several web bulletin boards.

It took a few more days, but I finally heard from someone who said he was Sileny Dumond, the Casino Services Director. Of course, I ended up having to re-explain the problem to him, and we exchanged a few emails before he began to see that it was not in his best interest to continue stringing me along.

It took 25 days from the time of my initial withdrawal request to the time that the money was credited back to my card. But I am convinced that it was only my vigorous efforts that got the results I was seeking. Meaning, I think they figure most players will assume the money was transferred, and won't take the time to follow up. In that case, the player forgets about the matter, and the casino keeps the money by default.

So, if you get flim-flammed, my advice is to follow up, and give them no peace until the matter is resolved. If necessary, write a letter with wording that is similar to the above.

Also, you can contact the National Fraud Information Center at www.fraud.org. Even if the matter is out of their jurisdiction, they might have some good tips.

SUMMARY OF
ONLINE WAGERING

At this writing, a million U.S. residents participate in online wagering every day, according to a recent article in the *New York Times*. But if you ask ten lawyers if doing so is legal, you might get ten different answers. Some say it's illegal, but not enforceable. Others will tell you that it varies from state to state. But if a state government could make the decision stick, why did the Nevada Gaming Commission hire a New York law firm to determine if their plan to legalize online gaming in Nevada would be allowable under federal law?

The Wire Act of 1961, which was designed to prohibit sports wagers over the phone, is, at this writing, the only existing federal law that could enforce penalties. But in legal circles, many doubt that this law is applicable, because it contains no specific mention of online gaming. And the more recent Kyl bill can't seem to make it through both houses of U.S. Congress, no matter how much the sponsors try to modify its language.

Nobody seems to know what to do. Everyone is waiting for the other guy to set the legal precedent, after which it is presumed that a national consensus will emerge. In the meantime, the players and the casinos keep chugging along, as if oblivious to the fact that there may be radical changes ahead.

What makes the issue unrelentingly complicated is the fact that most, if not all, online casinos are located outside the U.S., and therefore beyond state and federal jurisdiction. But most of these casinos, I understand, are owned and operated from the U.S. It's just the *servers* that are located offshore!

And it could be difficult for the U.S. government to try to get the cooperation of the Caribbean nations—where a lot of these servers are located—because the businesses have a very positive effect on their economies.

On the subject of online gaming, one thing you can be sure of, is that things can change fast. As this chapter was being written, it came to my attention that Microgaming, a company that supplies gaming software for online casinos, had just terminated its license to the Tropika group of casinos, because they were caught failing to make payoffs to players who won. And the software company has their reputation to protect. Julian Perry, a company spokesman, was quoted as saying: *There is no second chance. You can't refuse to pay winning players. The industry needs to be 100 percent fair and 100 percent whiter than white.*

The flagship casino in the Tropika group was called Fairplay. Other sites were Jetset, Magic Carpet, Aztec Gold, Orient Express, Iceberg, Astrobet, Bulls 'n Bears, Flying Dragon, Old Glory, and Bingotops. According to the article at rgtgaming.com, the software manufacturer *turned them off, because management does not have sufficient funds to pay the players, and no way can we ever let a casino misbehave.*

Around the same time, there was an online gaming scandal in Australia. It seems that an investigation confirmed that up to $30 million or more in dirty money (money associated with crime) was laundered in Australian web casinos.

And while that was going on, the state of New Jersey was in the process of suing three online casinos, which were based in the Caribbean, Costa Rica, and South Africa, for putting up billboard advertisements for their casinos in New Jersey. The reasoning was that casino gambling is legal only in Atlantic City, and the casinos were encouraging gambling by residents in other parts of the state. To entrap the casinos, state agents hired minors to pose as players, and the casinos were caught accepting wagers from them, without obtaining verification that they were of legal age.

All these things occurred in a three-week period. It just goes to show how fast things can change on the web.

From the player's point of view, however, the real issue here is whether online gaming provides a more efficient way to win, or a faster way to lose.

Legal questions aside, it's what you make it to be. Some will misunderstand the concept and think they've found the path to easy money, only to make a shocking discovery later on. Others will see it as an opportunity to play games of chance without having to bear the time and monetary costs that otherwise accompany a trip to a casino that has gaming tokens and free drinks.

Personally, I love online wagering. I love its accessibility and its efficiency. Now, there are times when I miss the atmosphere of a land casino, but I don't miss the crowds, the smoke-filled rooms, and the high table minimums during peak periods. And, of course, you've always got to watch your back in places like that. Not that casinos are a haven for crime, but you're definitely safer at home, than in a public place, carrying a lot of money.

One of the more positive points of online wagering is that the casinos characteristically offer deposit bonuses. The catch is that typically, you have to wager a substantial amount before you can lay claim to the bonus, but if you lose it, the money didn't come out of your pocket.

I hope you will take the advice offered at the beginning of the chapter, to check with the Internet Gaming Commission before you open an account with an online casino. If the casino you're looking up is not licensed, I suggest that you look elsewhere.

While online, I recommend that you check out Rolling Good Times, the online gaming magazine, at http://www.rgtgaming.com. This is where I got the news articles that were mentioned on the previous page, and it's the best source I know for gaming articles, news, and links.

And don't forget the Gambler's Book Shop, the world's best source for gaming books, at http://gamblersbookclub.com. They have the widest selection of gaming books on the planet.

Last: the addresses for two reputable online casinos, *Sands of the Caribbean* and *Intercasino,* are http://www.thesands.com and http://www.intercasino.com, respectively.

PART IV

THE
PSYCHOLOGICAL
ANGLES

14

THE PSYCHOLOGY OF
SUCCESSFUL PLAY

You've got to be constantly looking, and thinking.

—Sharon Pfeiffer

There is a specific mentality that is exclusively the dominion of the professional gambler. It is not easily found, but is easily lost. Because of the difficulty involved in acquiring and retaining this mindset, it is unlikely that you have ever met, or personally known, this rare breed of individual.

In playing this role, it's not just a matter of what you know; it's how you perceive things. You have to always be ready to make a bold move, but it must be executed with restraint. You've got to be constantly looking for hot bets, but you can't pursue them at the expense of losing your discipline.

How does the serious player reconciliate this paradoxical way of life? In this chapter, we'll take a look at the psychology behind the art of successful play.

SEEING THE BIG PICTURE

Chance favors the prepared mind.

—from *Under Seige II*

In a well-scripted drama, when a question is asked of one of the key players, there are times when it seems that he's answering the wrong question. And then the viewer realizes that he skipped ahead to the *end* question, which was several questions ahead of the one being asked!

He did so because he foresaw where the line of questioning was leading, and being a busy man, he didn't have time to waste on fruitless conversation. He had to move the matter along, and get right to the point.

It is this kind of big picture awareness that can make or break one's aspiration to be a successful gambler. You have to look past the obvious; beyond what all the others see, and be prepared for the result that no one else expected.

Seeing the big picture means switching from telephoto to the wide-angle lens. Stepping back a few paces, to see the larger view. Looking behind the façade, to see what is really the nature of the causative force.

The most successful players I've known all have three things in common:

1) They are highly focused on a specific goal.
2) No one else is doing what they're doing.
3) They are always mindful of the big picture.

Unfortunately, much of this type of awareness comes from experience. But if you stay alert and question everything you see, you'll get there a lot faster.

Quite a few years ago, while playing craps at Trump Plaza in Atlantic City, I was doing pretty well. I was betting the front line and winning most of my bets. But I decided to leave after reaching my very modest win goal. As I was standing near the table, trying to decide what to do next, I happened to overhear the conversation between two managers:

"Is this table *still* losing?"

With a look of chagrin, the other answered, "Yeah."

Suddenly realizing my error, I tried to get back to the spot I'd just left at the table. Too late. Someone else had grabbed my place. My bad. I had walked away from one of those tables that comes up only a few times in a player's lifetime.

But there's more to *big picture awareness* than just making an observation about which table to play. You have to think about what's going on with all your betting activity: yesterday, today, and tomorrow. You have to see the results of all your sessions as being part of a connected chain.

For example: it suddenly occurs to you that a 0 or 00 has not come up once in your last fifteen roulette sessions, which probably involved 150 table decisions. Now, *that* is a valuable piece of data. If you know a thing or two about the odds and statistics, you might conclude that hedges on the zeroes are positively a must in the foreseeable future.

When things you normally expect don't occur on schedule, take notice. The odds are changing. You can benefit from this, if you're savvy enough to know the probabilities, and then take the appropriate action.

And it doesn't matter if you're at a different table or casino. In the end, all the numbers fall neatly into place.

Seeing the big picture means piecing together all the fragments, so you can see what's going on behind the scenes. Use your imagination, be creative, and never forget that *eventually,* every number comes up. Even the number 5.

HORSE SENSE

Learning the art of gambling is very difficult. And, it is hard to find a book to properly teach it, because the numerical variations at most casino table games are nearly infinite. There are too many to document, or memorize.

In time, those who specialize in playing table games develop a sense of the best moves to make in any situation. This comes from seasoning and experience. Using the prior table patterns as a guide, they sense the *mood* of the table. They're not always right, but they maintain a winning percentage.

To reach into one's memory and recall a similar situation, then apply all the relevant data to the current challenge, requires a unique ability I call *horse sense.* But this is not something you can pick up in two weeks.

If the perfect system existed, there would be no need for this gift. But any seasoned player can tell you that gains acquired from using any system will ultimately be lost if you continue to play. What comes in must go back out.

People who buy gaming books are looking for a sage to show them The Magic Infallible Formula. But think about it: if anybody came through with that, it would be the last gaming book ever sold, and the end of casino gaming as we know it. Until the day comes when that book arrives, developing your own brand of horse sense is truly the best way.

If you want the accelerated program, you need to get to know the ways of the table. Study the patterns. Surround yourself with table results and statistics. This may sound like a lot of work, but technically, this is the shortcut!

PLAYING THE ODDS

At 5:05 AM, you pull off the Interstate and up to the traffic light at the end of the ramp. You're late for work, and you know this light has an ungodly long cycle. It's pitch black outside, and there are no other cars in sight. A few seconds later, you're pulling through the red light (!), and on down the road.

It was a snap decision, but you probably were not aware of the subconscious calculations you made in reaching it. You had assigned a (vague) rating to the probability of getting caught, and then acted on that impulse. This rating was likely derived from one or more of the categories below:

CATEGORY	APPROXIMATE PERCENTAGE	INTERPRETATION
1	0%	ZERO PROBABILITY
2	1% to 5%	EXTREMELY LOW PROBABILITY
3	6% to 20%	VERY LOW PROBABILITY
4	21% to 40%	LOW PROBABILITY
5	41% to 60%	AVERAGE PROBABILITY
6	61% to 80%	HIGH PROBABILITY
7	81% to 94%	VERY HIGH PROBABILITY
8	95% to 99%	EXTREMELY HIGH PROBABILITY
9	100%	ABSOLUTE CERTAINTY

FIGURE 47
The Range of Probabilistic Expectations

You weren't thinking of a precise number at the time, but mentally, you had assigned a probability in the vicinity of category 2 or 3. Your projection that you could get away with it turned out to be correct.

I doubt that many people are aware of the probabilities they calculate in virtually everything they do, but this process is what helps us make decisions. It's a natural part of getting through this thing we call life.

What are the chances that you'll get lucky on your date tonight? If there is a reasonable chance to begin with, you might be able to push the number up a notch or two if you're generous, well groomed, and polite.

What are the odds that you'll get mugged when you visit the ATM machine late at night on a deserted corner? Or that someone will run off with the SUV you leave running while you dash in to the convenience store? If you want to avoid adverse swings of fortune, you have to be aware of the downside.

Any chance that the headache medicine you just bought contains cyanide, put there by a prankster? The odds are real low on that, but they're not zero!

We all play the odds, every day and in everything we do. How well we appraise upcoming events helps determine the level of success we can attain. Which means that the best guessers are the biggest winners.

But it's not so much guesswork as it is deduction.

How do you hone these skills? You have to think about what has happened 1) lately, and 2) over a longer span of time. From there, try to weave the two together into a single fabric. In doing this, you must consider a proportionate weight to confer to each of the categories. Most times, a slightly higher value should be given to the late-breaking results, because they could represent a trend that's still in progress.

In effect, you're using information gleaned from past events to help you extrapolate future results.

As they say, the more you know, the luckier you get.

Play the odds. Play to win.

RESISTANCE, ARIZONA

You're trying out a new roulette strategy, and the results are astounding. After winning 27 of your first 30 sessions, there is no doubt in your mind that this is the one that will make you rich! While trying to decide between getting the Mercedes or the Ferrari, you play a few more sessions for fun.

Hello, what's this? Suddenly, you can't pull out a win to save your life. The system that was so wonderful for so long has turned to Death Valley Dust. What happened?

Then you see the signpost: "Welcome to Resistance, Arizona: The most Godforsaken place on Earth. Population: 1."

If you should experience the gift of amazing luck while doing anything that even remotely pertains to gaming, don't let yourself be fooled. Eventually, the other shoe will drop.

How? Why? Well, you just happened to hit a blissful moment when whatever you were doing was in perfect sync with the tables. And you caught a passing trend. That's all.

I admit, seeing something turn to pure crud, after working so marvelously for so long, is downright surreal.

If you play any strategy long enough, there will always come a day when it's nothing but endless blue skies, and another day when it's blacker than black.

The message: the luckier you get at the tables, the more you tempt the downside to pounce on you will lethal force, just to show you who's in charge.

Awareness of that place called *Resistance, Arizona* will help keep you from being set up by an insidious table trend. Think of it as another one of the many fun facts of gaming.

THE HIERARCHY OF CHESS

In the early 1980s, I worked as a Designer in the Space and Communications division of Hughes Aircraft in L.A. There was a rivalry going on between the third and fifth floors of the building I was in, relating to the company volleyball matches. The fifth floor (my floor) was taking regular drubbings from the third floor, and I stepped forward to attempt to singlehandedly redeem our floor's reputation. I put up a notice that challenged anyone from the third floor to beat me in a three-game chess match. And to emphasize the point, I offered to put up $100 against $20 from the contender, toward a winner-take-all pot of $120. That is, I was offering 5 to 1 odds to anyone who could beat me.

I soon learned that Hughes Aircraft did not permit that sort of gambling on the premises. The notice had to be taken down, but word of the offer spread. By the next day, a challenger had been identified. It was arranged for the monetary side of the offer to be handled discreetly, through a third party.

Who could this challenger be, I wondered. I thought I knew the approximate skill level of all the third floor chess players, and I was confident that none of them could whip me. But then I learned who it was. It seems that there was an engineer in one of the back offices who was officially rated a Master, and in fact, his name was published in a chess magazine as being the 33rd best player in the state of California!

Later, the department head, Gary Kenworthy, met me in the hall and wished me luck, but I told him that there was no chance for me to win. "Why not?" he asked.

"If you understood the hierarchy of chess," I said, "you'd know that I'm dead meat."

He looked at me quizzically.

"When you get to the level that *he's* at," I continued, "beating someone who is rated 500 points below him is like the proverbial candy from a baby. I can't touch him."

Gary shrugged and walked away, not quite getting it, which was understandable for a non-player.

The day of the match came, and in a desperate move to throw my rival off balance, I opened with the King's Gambit, a flawed strategy which can sometimes be effective against a player who is not expecting it. It seemed to be working for a while, but I ended up resigning after 40 moves. In retrospect, I'm proud to have lasted that long against such a player!

In my second game, I lasted only 20 moves. Bye-bye $100. So much for my attempt to vindicate the fifth floor.

I mention this because I want to convey what happened to me during the match. First, understand that some high-ranking Hughes employees were there to watch this, and also, some women whom I wanted very badly to impress. Because of that, and the fact of the money that was on the line, I felt such mental pressure during that match that I had never felt before. My head was throbbing, and when I got up at the end, I was walking like a drunk. Now, I had heard about the intense mental pressure of the International chess matches, but could not grasp the concept until that day when I tried to "save the fifth floor."

The point is, when *meaningful* money is at stake, your body goes through physiological changes you can't control. Your heart beats faster; you sweat, and your head pounds like a jackhammer. This takes a while to get used to.

Same goes for online wagering. Let's say I'm surfing the net, visiting the Lord of the Rings site, and I remember that I had meant to play a few roulette sessions to beef up my player's account. Suddenly, right after the thought occurred to me, I feel a little bit queasy. I feel a sense of dread. Now that's odd. Just a moment ago, I felt fine.

Here's the tip of the week: if you're in the habit of putting money on the line, be prepared for the side effects.

THE COMFORT ZONE

You have to know your situation and tailor a plan to fit both your goals and your comfort level.

—Peter Lynch, Fidelity Investments
(speaking on the subject of investing)

It is your very first visit to a casino, but you feel adequately prepared. You have devoured several gaming books from cover to cover, and performed studies on paper that indicate the likelihood of success with the strategy you intend to use.

You buy in for $100, and after just forty minutes of play, you cash out with $60 profit. Everything is going according to plan. Now comes the fun part: projecting how much you would've made if you had been playing at a higher level.

Playing with blacks ($100 chips) instead of reds ($5 chips) would have represented a twenty-fold increase in your winnings. That works out to $1200. Not a bad rate of pay for forty minutes of work. Now, all you've got to do is build up your bankroll, and you can be making the big money.

Hold up there, Sport. One session does not a career make. And, you can't assume that you could handle playing with the big money, even if you had it in the first place.

At the nickel level, you were doing fine once you got past the first four bets, which were losses. But if you had been playing with the blacks, you'd have been out $400 instead of $20. The question of the day is: would you have done the same thing at that point, as you did with the red chips?

The odds against that, I'm afraid, are higher than the flagpole on top of the Empire State Building. And while there *are* higher structures around, it *is* high enough to mean that the $1200 figure you derived from your conversion would be bogus.

This is what happens when you play outside that venerable perimeter known as the *comfort zone*. Reaching your ideal betting level is something that must be worked towards in stages. You're not going to make it in a single bound. Well, you might actually get there, but you won't last.

I speak from experience. This very problem has plagued me from day one, and remains a problem today. I could be making so much more if I could overcome it. But doing so would require that —to some extent—I adopt a reckless attitude towards my money, which is not easy to do. I work too hard for it. It means too much to me to treat it with such disrespect.

With some strategies, graduating to higher bet levels involves a simple routine of substituting larger bets, and stepping through the procedure. At times, however, I can maintain a higher win rate with freestyle betting, which requires a heavy reliance on instinct. This not only tells me *what* to bet, but also, *how much* that bet is worth. In an exact dollar figure. And when I go messing with that, it throws me off my game.

In other words, when you stray from your instinct, you lose sight of what you would have done under normal circumstances, which causes you to lose the mentality that was helping you win. For the remainder of the session, you are unable to reconstruct that state of mind.

And all I have addressed so far are the *internal* influences. There are quite a few external influences that come into play when you start betting larger. For one thing, your play will come under more scrutiny by the casino. And you'll always wonder if one of the players is cooking up a scheme to assault you after you leave. That has never happened to me, but the possibility can weigh on one's mind. It's a bit disconcerting.

I wish it weren't so, but dealing with your comfort zone is one more obstacle between you and the big money.

THE IMPORTANCE OF A LOW PROFILE

Try to look unimportant. The enemy may be low on ammo and not want to waste a bullet on you.

—from *The Fax Review*

If you have a serious intention to use your skill at gaming as a means of generating income, you have to consider the amount of resistance that will come into play. The basic rule of thumb is this: the more money you want to make, the harder the journey will be. Part of the reason for this is the limitations imposed by the comfort zone, as was just discussed. But there are other problems that arise, which can't be avoided.

In this line of work, one thing you should never forget is that your gains are causing someone else, somewhere, to lose. And you should trust me on this, pal: nobody likes to lose. And nobody is going to allow such a condition to continue unchallenged forever, if they have the means to stop it.

What can the casino do? You might be surprised at what they can come up with when there's money at stake.

Remember, a casino is first and foremost a business. Seldom is their cash flow at risk, but when it is, they have the clout, and intelligence, to find a creative way to protect themselves. And that may include barring a player (who has a habit of winning) from the casino, or from certain games.

A professional understands the importance of maintaining a low profile, so as not to jeopardize the privilege of making money in a casino.

For the most part, it's simply a matter of discretion. If at all possible, don't give them your name, and don't use credit. Spread your action around to different casinos and different work shifts. Make extra sure the same floorperson doesn't see you winning too much, too often.

Casinos present themselves as places where the good times roll, and money is recklessly exchanged, but if you look closely, you'll see that it's the customers only, and not them, who are the reckless ones.

Some years ago while staying at Lake Tahoe, I financed the trip with my earnings from playing minibaccarat. While at a table in Harrah's, a middle-aged Asian gentleman took a seat at my table and asked for a marker for $2000. While that was being processed, he asked the floorperson if they could raise the table limit from $1000 to $2000. The floorperson politely told him he didn't have the authority to do so, but after a quick phone call, the limit was raised. I watched in amazement as this man started shucking and grinding, first with stacks of greens, and then stacks of black chips. In a few minutes, he was making $1200 bets with the blacks, and it didn't bother him in the least when he lost one of those big bets. He looked bored, as if he was just killing time while his wife was playing the slots, or getting a pedicure.

Thirty minutes after arriving, he left the table with $7800 in value chips, which was *after* paying off the marker. Once he was gone, I was at the table to see the look of apology on the dealer's face as she talked it over with the floorperson.

The next day that table was shut down. There was, in fact, no minibaccarat action in the whole casino. I asked when a table would open, and was told *Noon*. But it never happened. And three days later, when I left Lake Tahoe, there had been no change in the situation.

To this day, I wish I knew where he learned his technique. But it doesn't matter, because I don't like burning bridges I may some day want to use. For although he did good, the goose with the golden eggs was now dead and gone.

To me, that's too steep a price for a one-time victory.

BATTLING BACK

The slow turtle gets made into soup.

—Glen Bedel

One of the things I particularly like about online betting is the fact that these days, some of my sessions only last a minute or so. Sometimes, all I'm seeking is one good win, and if I get it on my first bet, I'm done. No way could I do that in a land-based casino, because I'd have to play longer, and earn more, to justify the time and expense involved with making the trip.

But it's not always that easy. There are times when a session erupts into a fierce battle, after which one must dig himself out of a hole. And if I didn't know how to do that, I would have no chance at all for long range success.

The art of *battling back* involves accepting the fact that your original plan did not work, and consequently, you have to lower your sights and play more conservatively. This is in contrast to the approach used by many fledgling players, which is to try to force a win by pouring money onto the problem. This, by the way, is the worst mistake a player can make.

Perhaps it will work out differently for you, but I feel that the only way you have a chance to make it as a successful player is to specialize in battling back. Learn how to dig yourself out of a hole. Squeeze out a win the hard way, if necessary.

This is an extension of the lesson conveyed on page 7:

*To be able to win, you must first know how to **not lose.***

This is a fundamental precept of successful play, and the key to learning how to overcome a disadvantaged position.

Example: you go to a casino, and play the strategy that has in recent history been working very well for you. But for whatever reason, things are not coming together today. You've played only two sessions, towards which you invested $100 apiece, but now you're $200 in the hole. What do you do?

Immediately, you have to change your tack. It is no longer a *business as usual* situation. From this moment forward, all of your thought and effort must go toward making sure that you contain the damage. Your focus is no longer on winning. Now, your prime objective is to *not lose*.

This means you have to be more tentative, and more careful. You don't want to abandon your technique, but you will have to be more sensitive to which way the winds of fortune are blowing. You must be more prepared to bail out in your next session, against the possibility that your bad luck will continue.

Also, at that point, you must acknowledge that, for reasons beyond your control or understanding, you may have little hope to win today, no matter what you do. It may be best to swallow your loss, and turn to other (non-gaming) matters.

The reason for all this, is that you must not jeopardize your most precious asset: your bankroll. This is your toolkit. This is the bag of goodies that enables you to do your job. Without it, you're unable to function. You can't work, because you don't have the means to complete the task.

But this is much more serious than just losing one's tools, because that which comprises your bankroll is the same stuff that keeps you alive: money.

So, losing your bankroll not only puts your employment at risk; it also endangers your survival on this planet.

This is what has to be going through your mind when a day at the tables starts to turn bad. From the first moment things go amiss, the red flag should be run up the pole.

This is the mentality I call *battling back*. A large part of it is having the wisdom to know you're overmatched, and retreating into the mist. To conserve your resources so that you will live to fight another battle, on another day.

WHAT IT TAKES TO WIN

You never win when you need it most.

—Elissa Gough

Now that you have some idea how to *not lose,* we can take a serious look at what it takes *to win.*

In many movies where gambling is depicted, you often see the key players taking reckless chances at the tables. In one such James Bond movie, *Diamonds Are Forever,* you have to follow the plot closely to be aware that it's not his money that's put at risk. So, many of the viewers, I imagine, leave the theater with the false impression that this is how he normally plays.

It's nice to dream, but Hollywood has a way of exaggerating the glamour of a situation. So, one has to take this distortion of the truth with a grain of salt.

Well then, what sort of picture accurately depicts the way a successful gambler wins, and continues to win? And what did it take for him to get there in the first place?

The concept is actually quite simple: go for small gains, until your winnings enable you to go for larger gains.

With every bet you make, you must stay focused on your end goal of being able to continue the effort. Meaning, protecting your bankroll is your top priority. What complicates the task, however, is the hardship of dealing with losses. It's always nice to win, but the losses send a very powerful message: at that moment in time, you're a loser. It hurts. You're upset. You want to retaliate. You want to prove to the world that this is just a fluke. You can win; you just need more time. More bets.

The people who run the casinos know of this effect on the people who play their games. They know that the wins are taken in stride, but they don't compensate the pain of losing. Consequently, the player tends to become obsessed with the idea that he has to get back his losses immediately.

This is why the casinos win.

A disciplined player sees his wins and losses as nothing more than table decisions that have an equal value. He knows he has to sustain a given number of losses over a certain period of time; he does not begrudge them. They are a necessary part of the picture. He knows that every group of losses he sustains brings him that much closer to a flurry of wins. And so he ignores the insult, and keeps playing his game, the same as before. He always comes back with a *measured* response.

For the inexperienced player, this is harder than it sounds, because your brain is sending you signals that you need to get back at the table that did that to you. And it's urgent.

To succeed, however, you have to rise above that mentality. You are the one in control. Not the table; not the casino; not the statistics. You will emerge victorious in the end, and the victory will be on your terms. Until you learn to see it that way, I suspect that you'll be a fat target.

At the top of the previous page was the quote: *You never win when you need it most.* This was spoken by a friend of mine when we last visited the Belterra riverboat. Those words underscore the point that there is no place for emotion in a casino. You can't ever pinpoint when the wins will come; you just have to play your game and take what the tables give you. If suddenly you decide that you *need to win,* it is almost a dead certainty that from that moment forward, you'll do nothing but lose!

This is one of the many paradoxes of player-side gaming: the more you need to win, the greater the chance you'll lose.

When the table deals you a tough loss, best thing to do is to leave the table and cool off. Turn your thoughts to other matters. The table didn't do that to you on purpose.

Take it in stride. Move on.

HOW MUCH
CAN YOU MAKE?

The only way to discover the limits of the possible is to go beyond them into the impossible.

—Clarke's Second Law

Back when I was young and foolish, I came upon the notion that if I could learn how to make $5 a day in a casino *consistently,* then—simply by going to larger bets—I could make $5000 a day. If necessary, I could do it in stages.

If you have been paying attention throughout this book, you would know that it's not that simple. As I said earlier, all kinds of complications can come into play when you try to maximize your success by betting larger.

For starters, you have to obtain proof that you can continue to win as you did before. Just because you've shown a profit from your last fifty sessions does not guarantee that the next fifty will be as easy. Games of chance have a way of dishing out their biggest surprises when least expected.

Then there's the comfort zone to contend with. It takes time and seasoning to adjust to higher betting levels.

Another thing to consider is bankroll. To support the effort to make $5000 a day, you'd probably need a wagering fund in the neighborhood of $100,000. And that's the low bid. Chances are, you'd need more than that.

One of your biggest problems, however, is that your play will come under intense scrutiny. Casino management will be watching every move you make.

Remember, somebody is bearing the cost of your wins. And that's the sort of thing that people notice. It matters not if you're playing a 'negative expectation game.' If you're taking away their money on a consistent basis, it's just a matter of time before they intervene. Sure, they expect a few players to win occasionally, but they're not in business to give money away.

In addition to all that has been described so far, there is one more obstacle to making the big bucks that is seldom discussed in books. This pertains to a condition that you may never understand until you are doing it: when you live the life of constantly putting your money at risk, it takes a toll. Every single day, it seems that everything you own is put on the chopping block. It's a day-to-day scrap for survival, and tomorrow, it could all disappear in a wisp of purple smoke.

There is no sense of permanence in what you've acquired, because you don't know if you can keep the gains you've worked so hard to accumulate. Tomorrow, or the next day, you could slip and fall, all the way to the bottom. And it's a long way down, and a longer way back up.

When everything you do involves money and numbers, it gets tedious, and frightening. Even the most weathered practitioner of the game never feels like he can relax if there's more money to put on the line before the day is out.

So, there's little desire to make any more today than the exact amount you need, because you know that in trying to get that little bit more, you could, conceivably, end up losing all your gains from the past week. For this reason, the most cherished moment in your day will be when you quit playing, because finally, you don't have to put any more money at risk.

When you stop, all the anxiety suddenly slips away, and you are at peace with the world. Your profit for the day is locked up. They can't take it away from you, because you know it's not going to be put at risk!

So, even though you have the skill to make more money, you learn to be content with less.

As Mies Van Der Rohe once said, *less is more.*

BANKROLL SAFEGUARDS

Life will be rosy. . .if you can just get out of this one silly little jam.

—Evelyn Marsh,
from *Twin Peaks*

In trying to make a point—on the previous page—about the dangers of putting one's money at risk, I may have overstated the problem just a tad. I wanted to make sure the message got through, but in fact there are ways to protect yourself against the possibility of blowing your wad in a moment of weakness.

Enter *bankroll safeguards*. Initiatives that hinder your ability to access too much of your money too quickly. Measures that you put into place to prevent you from draining your bank accounts if you should suffer a serious lapse of discipline.

Can't happen to you? Perhaps not, if you are an occasional player. But if you are serious about making a living in this way, I hope you will trust me in saying that by virtue of being human, you have the capacity to do this.

It shouldn't be hard to incorporate your own safeguards, but the matter should be addressed before doing any serious gambling. For starters, avoid high-stakes poker games, because verbal bets are assumed to be binding. This is where people can lose things like cars, and houses—in a single bet.

You may have your own ideas about how to do this, but your end goal should be to give yourself only as much spending power as you think you can stand to lose in a day.

That way, you won't hate yourself in the morning.

ALIENS IN THE GAMING AREA

As I have said in the past, one has to expect the unexpected while at the tables, because anything can happen. Example: you're playing roulette at the Luxor, when suddenly, a band of hostile aliens busts into the room and starts zapping the players with laser beams coming out of their eyes.

What do you do?

I know this sounds a little over the top, because the odds of winning the Powerball Lotto are much lower, but in keeping with my policy to keep gamesters in tune with every contingency, I've compiled the following list:

WHAT TO DO WHEN EVIL ALIENS APPEAR IN THE GAMING AREA:

1) Grab your high value chips, drop down under the table, and look away.
2) Avoid eye contact.
3) If the creatures have no eyes, avoid *all* contact.
4) If you get out alive, scrub all body parts with cleanser.
5) If anyone asks, this never happened.

Please, folks, don't make the mistake that Bernie Tibbsky, of Peanut Falls, Idaho, did the last time this happened. He didn't have any Ajax on hand, so he tried mixing some ammonia with chlorine bleach, not realizing he was creating deadly chlorine gas. He won't be making *that* mistake again!

Obviously, if this happens while you're playing online, there is a whole different set of rules. First off, there probably won't be any other people around to serve as the first victims, which might satiate the aliens' appetite for the obligatory amount of death and destruction that usually accompanies a drop-in visit. Chances are good that you'll be trapped in your room at home, with the alien blocking the egress.

If this is the case, your only chance may be to reason with the sunuvabitch, which won't be easy. Some of the more obscure races of aliens communicate by wiggling whatever appendage happens to be in the vicinity of their heads. Try to be sensitive to this. Then, see if you can distract him long enough to make a getaway. If you make it out in one piece, run like hell.

Most important, keep your voice from getting too shrill, and don't get him (or it) upset.

If all else fails, kick him in the crotch (if he's got one). But if you try this, you gotta be fast!

Now, if you do manage to get away, but you can't get him out of your home, DO NOT try to handle the matter yourself. This is something that should be left to the experts. Check the yellow pages under "UFO Removal Services" and see if you can get a good price. If there aren't any companies like that in your town, you may have to get the authorities involved. But only do that as a last resort, because those guys will probably want to put yellow tape all around your property, and they'll be removing all sorts of "evidence" from the premises.

Of course, taking that option means that you can't explicitly follow Rule Number 5 from the list, because it will be obvious that you really did have a close encounter.

But that's okay, because it will be the authorities who start the conversation in that direction. The point of Rule Number 5 is to keep the rest of the world from thinking you're a nut case because you were the only one who saw the aliens.

Like I've always said, gaming is a tricky business. You never know what can happen.

THE WAY I PLAY

Everyone has talent; what is rare is the courage to follow the talent to the dark place where it may lead.

—Erica Jong

If player-side gaming wasn't such a complex issue, I could tell my readers how it is *I* play, and let them sink or swim. But my technique is mostly a matter of style, which can be imitated—not duplicated. Also, it would be unrealistic to expect my readers to play at an advanced level too soon.

I would, however, like to try to give you a sense of what I'm seeking, and what I try to do when I play. Perhaps this can serve as a guide for where to take aim.

These days, virtually all of my play is online. The only time I go to a land-based casino is when someone talks me into going, or I'm on vacation, or, for my ongoing research. As I've been hinting throughout this book, I'm only in it for the money. I don't get my kicks from the glitter.

At this time, the two strategies I play regularly are Targeted Sixlines and the 3Q/A. Lately, I've been favoring the T6, because I've been having good luck with it, and you want to go where the good luck persists, even if it happens to be towards the weakest of the two strategies you usually play. See, there's more to successful gambling than just picking the biggest, baddest club in your bag, and then start swinging away. No, you're better off if you stay in tune with where the wins are coming from at that precise moment, and then following that lead. But only in the big picture sense. You can't go chasing after every whim.

But I don't want to mislead you. It's not so much *favoring* a certain strategy, as it is letting the table make the choice.

At the start of a recent 3Q/A session, the qualifying numbers contained four A numbers and zero 3Q numbers. Technically, I'm supposed to play the 3Q in that situation, but I prefer to see at least one number from the group I'm supposed to play in the qualifying five. Since there isn't one, I check off the sixlines that have hit, per the targeted sixlines strategy, and I see that the table is primed for me to play the second and fourth sixline. So I shoot my bets in that direction, and I get a win on the second bet.

All I'm doing here is looking for the path of least resistance. As I see it, there's no point in making the task any harder than it needs to be.

In the matter of choosing which casino to play, what I have found to be effective is to play these two strategies at two online casinos, in a way that sort of pits the one casino against the other, as a way of circumventing a losing streak. I can't say much more about it, except that it simulates the effect of moving from table to table, as one might do in a land casino.

Last month, I was more into freestyle wagering, which can be more challenging, but also more rewarding. And next month I may go back to it, or something else altogether. My point in saying this is to drive a point home: don't keep doing the same thing forever. If you don't mix it up, the tables will get your number. They'll all start conspiring against you, and when that happens, buddy, you got trouble! Well, it's not quite like that, but in reality, no matter what you play, if it is played exclusively, you're going to hit that beastie of a table that will rock your world!

Why make yourself vulnerable to that? You're really better off if you keep your strikes brief, and varied. That way, when the skies cloud up, you can head for shelter. There's no point in trying to weather a storm if you can dodge it altogether!

The above pertains to my experiences with online wagering, but the words also apply to gambling in a joint with the carpeting, marble columns, and chandeliers.

Just don't forget which one is which.

SUMMARY: THE PSYCHOLOGY OF SUCCESSFUL PLAY

Everything should be made as simple as possible, but no simpler.

—from *The Fax Review*

When dealing with a situation where the stakes are high, your human qualities can get in the way of your goals. Your head, your heart, and your nervous system go through changes that you can't control. But the biggest obstacle you face is the tricks your mind will play. It's sending you signals which must be suppressed on a continuous basis.

The people who run casinos are masters at the exploitation of these weaknesses of the human spirit, which adds yet another level of difficulty to the task at hand.

The best defense against this is to be aware of these effects, and take whatever measures you can to combat them. Beyond that, it wouldn't hurt to keep one eye on Murphy's Law whenever you visit a casino. Meaning, be on guard at all times. Expect the worst result at the worst possible moment.

Also, don't underestimate the power of trends. If you spend much time in a casino—online or off—you're going to see things you won't believe. It's as if the table truly has a mind of its own. What you're seeing is nothing more than a numerical aberration, but it will be hard to convince yourself that those *really are* just random table patterns you're seeing.

But all this is what makes it the challenge that it is!

PART V

PUTTING IT ALL TOGETHER

15

GETTING STARTED

Whatever you can do, or dream you can do, begin it.

—von Goethe

In most endeavors, *getting started* is the biggest challenge of all. This is especially true in matters pertaining to the exploitation of games of chance.

The first obstacle you will face is that you haven't yet built up a monetary reserve, but this is not something that money alone can solve. Even if you have the money, it wasn't *won* money. It's more precious to you, because you know how hard you worked to get it. And, you haven't the confidence that comes from knowing that you got it by beating the casinos.

Because of this, you have to do things more tentatively on the front end than after you've found your stride. It will be harder for you to bear losses caused by flukes—like putting your chips on the wrong sixline, or getting whacked by the 00 in three straight bets. Little things like that are going to hurt you, and could cause you to change your game plan.

And so, a difficult task becomes that much harder.

If you are serious about making money in casinos, the first thing to do is to get some scorecards printed up, so you can start collecting your own database of table results. These can be used to make projections of how a strategy will perform in a live situation. Never throw these table results away!

After you get your scorecards, you need to focus on honing your gaming skills through practice. This task is simplified if you have access to the Internet, because there are many online casinos that offer practice modes. *Intercasino* and *Sands of the Caribbean* are two that offer both live and free play modes. If you don't have web access, you can purchase a system tester at a bookstore, and use that data to simulate live gaming results.

When you lose a series in a practice game, stop playing for a while—as you would do in real life. Move away from the table and spend a few minutes doing something else. This is more important than you might think. To be truly prepared, you need to go through the same motions that you would encounter in the real world. This helps condition you toward the right habits.

When you start playing live bets, your focus should be more on what you can learn from that experience, than on how much money you can make. Keep your sessions short, so you'll have the time to analyze the results, rate the performance of your strategy, and evaluate your own performance.

Accept the fact that mistakes will be made. Try to learn the reasons they occurred, and ponder how to avoid them in the future. After you've mastered them, however, don't be surprised if new ones move to the front.

Acclimating yourself to this life is best done by keeping your sessions brief, then assessing that experience. Little by little, you'll gain a better understanding of what you're up against, and what you have to do. At some point, you will feel ready to take larger risks, by playing more aggressively. Just don't stick your neck out too far. One troubling observation I have made is that whenever I decide to go for larger stakes, disaster is not far behind, waiting to crush my spirit.

Nothing is easy. Least of all, this!

BUILDING A BANKROLL

When you're new, you take your time, you build up, you learn.

—Laila Ali

The first thing you should know about building a bankroll is that it is much, much easier to do on the web than in a land casino. Online, you don't have the travel expenses, the crowds to fight, the pressure to bet within a set timeframe, or the high table minimums. And apart from all that, it also saves time.

True, online wagering cannot capture the ambience of a real casino, nor can you get a great deal on a buffet dinner in your den. But my words are directed toward those who see the casino games as instruments for leveraging income. If you fall into that category, you've found the right page.

Things being what they are, a wagering fund of $300 should be adequate for playing European roulette with $1 table minimums online, at a site like *Sands of the Caribbean.* But if you want to try your luck in a brick-and-mortar casino, I would suggest a starting bank of no less than $2000.

The primary reason for the disparity between these two sets of figures is the table minimums. While most land casinos have $5 tables, they are not usually abundant, and, are packed with players during peak periods. This means that you'll be stuck playing at $10 tables most of the time. That's ten times the figure for the online casino mentioned above, which accounts for the need of a larger fund. And that doesn't count the travel expenses you will incur, which should not come out of your bankroll.

For online wagering, I should make it clear that you won't be playing just $1 bets. The 3Q/A, for example, calls for coverage on three quad bets, or two sixlines. For that, you'll have a minimum outlay of either $2 or $3. But the 3Q/A is stronger than most (if not all) strategies that are out there, so you should get by with $300 as a starting bank. If you exhaust that amount, I would tend to think that the rules were not strictly followed.

In a land casino, there will probably be similar impediments to keeping your bets at $10. For one thing, a three-unit bet like the 3Q does not divide into ten, so you'll have to use a $12 bet as your base. Now, you *can* get around this if you hedge, by putting $3 on each quad and $1 on the 0–00 split. That works out to an even $10, and being a hedge bettor myself, I recommend it.

These wagering funds will serve as your temporary bankroll while you are accumulating the capital to form the real thing. After you reach your goal, you should put the borrowed money back to where you got it.

How big should your bankroll be? Ideally, you should have enough money to ride out a hundred consecutive losses, at the level you have established as the norm.

How many sessions should be allowed for within a bankroll? At least ten. In a land casino, your buy-in should be $100 to $200. If you win 30% to 40%, or lose 50% to 70% of your buy-in, it's time to end the session. In each case, start packing your gear when you hit the first of those two figures.

Online, you won't be making a buy-in, because you use the funds in your player's account. This convenience, however, is one of the negative aspects of online wagering: your entire bankroll is in full view and accessible. And that doesn't provide the same kind of natural barrier that you have when—in a land-based casino—you start running out of chips.

It would be great if these online casinos let you store some of your accumulated gains in a separate account, so you could go into a session with only as much money as what was predetermined. But this would interfere with the casino profits, and besides, most of their clientele are recreational players.

What this means, is that when playing online, you have to be more careful to establish your win and loss limits in advance, and make sure you stick to them. Having said that, though, I'm fairly certain that most of my readers will blow their first online bankroll because of some kind of lapse of discipline. That's another reason I'm suggesting a smaller amount for playing online: to help contain your losses!

Won't happen to you? Perhaps not, but it would be best for you to be prepared for the possibility. It might help if you picture in your mind how you would feel after losing the entire $300 in just fifteen minutes, and then make a solemn vow not to let that happen, but I can't say that even that would help. The tables have a way of tugging at your emotions, and inciting behavorial patterns you didn't know you had.

If and when you get past the bankroll-blowing stage, your goal is to keep the money coming in, a little at a time. There will be losses to deal with periodically, but you want for the overall earnings curve to have an upward slant.

If you're playing in a land casino, be prepared for all kinds of interference. For example: you see a playable situation at a table, but you can't get your bet down in time because it's too late in the spin. Or, some lady is spreading out last-minute chips like she's sowing grass seed, and her hovering hand blocks you from putting your chips on the desired target. Or, what was a $10 table twenty minutes ago now has a $25 minimum.

And don't forget the old classic, which is Ellison's Sixth Law of Gaming: *If you misplace a chip, the spot where it was supposed to go will be the winning number, every time.* That is technically an exaggeration, but I hope you see my point.

Building a bankroll is an ongoing process of taking so many steps forward, then so many back. Forward; back. Forward; back. It takes a special kind of person to deal with the all the reversals that take place.

But it's not unlike being an insurance agent. There's a steady stream of money coming in, but every so often a hurricane comes along and wipes those gains away!

THE FIVE RULES

A crisis is when you can't say "Let's forget the whole thing."

—from *The Fax Review*

On the preceding pages, two sets of figures were mentioned as goals for establishing a bankroll: $300 for online gaming, and $2000 for live casino play. But what do you do when you exhaust this fund? Do you give up, or set up another fund?

I wouldn't advise anyone to keep investing in something that proves to be a constant drain on his resources. If this is happening, you may have to take a hard look at whether or not you are suited for this type of endeavor.

If, however, you think you're learning from your mistakes, and believe you can do better in the future, here are some operating guidelines which should be beneficial:

RULE 1: *When the tables give you a hard time, settle for whatever you can get.* Don't fight too hard, because you are not yet a match for such a cunning adversary. Think of yourself as a thief, stealing jewels from the dragon's lair. Be thankful that you got out of there alive!

RULE 2: *Keep your goals modest. You're not seeking a big score.* Start out by testing the water to see if you can get a bite. If every chip you toss out sinks straight to the bottom, you should acknowledge that this is not a good sign. Drop what you're doing, and move on to another table.

What you're doing is like jumping onto a speeding train. At first, all you're trying to do is hang on and try to keep up with the flow of things. When you start getting regular returns, you'll know you're keeping pace with the table, for the moment. From there, try to get a feel for its destination.

RULE 3: *When you're winning, move in slowly for the kill.* This is why you came: to catch the trend that is completely in sync with you. Don't make any drastic changes to what you're doing, but also beware of overconfidence. Cash out at the first sign of trouble.

Note: this rule was meant to apply to an ongoing session, as opposed to a surgical strike. In the case of the latter, you want to be sensitive to how you're doing in general.

RULE 4: *When that inevitable losing jag arrives, don't let yourself be swayed by other temptations.* If everything you do is coming up—shall we say—the opposite of roses, take some time out and do something else for a while. Depending on how bad it is, you have two choices: try again later, or, quit for the day. If you're experiencing a lot of resistance, it may be best to accept the likely fact that this just isn't your day to win.

Most important, don't get discouraged to the point that you head for the blackjack tables, because you were desperate to find a game *where you could win.*

RULE 5: *Remember, if you maintain your discipline, you cannot fail in the long run.* This is really all it comes down to: can you avoid losing your discipline? If you can, there is no reason you can't succeed. If you don't, well, that's it.

What this means is that you must never lose your cool. Never respond to the anger or emotion you may feel. And never think that you're unbeatable.

These five rules aren't all you need to make it, but if you can remember them, you'll be way ahead of the pack.

THE BUSINESS PLAN

There is no shortcut to results when you're a pro.

—GMC commercial

The shortest path to success as a player of casino table games is to regard that endeavor as a business. And as is the case with any other business, you must have complete information as to what you are getting into. This involves some thought and investigation, to help you project figures which represent the relative probabilities of success, and failure. The only way to get this information is to assemble a business plan.

In forming a business plan that is customized to your needs and preferences, you should think about what you've seen in this book—and elsewhere—that appeals to you. If nothing comes to mind, it might help if you re-read chapters 9 through 13, with that objective in mind. As you read, think about how you would feel playing this strategy or that strategy. Do you like playing favorites, or do you prefer longshots? Perhaps you'd like a mix. That's fine. All that matters is that you pin something down, to give yourself a starting point.

Most of my readers, I imagine, will choose the 3Q/A as their first choice, since it is statistically the strongest of all those that are presented herein. But it is best to have more than one road to take. This will enable you to exit the freeway and take an alternate route when you see congestion ahead.

But this raises the question: why would anyone elect to play a weaker strategy than the one being played?

The answer to this lies in the cold, hard truth that no strategy or business is immune to bad luck. The most stable and profitable businesses in the world, including banks, insurance companies and the casinos themselves, occasionally go bankrupt—because of an unlikely bad run of statistical variance.

And so it is with gaming strategies. No matter which one you choose, if you play it exclusively, the day will come when you hit a table where everything you do is wrong. And you can't escape it. Moving to another table won't help. You're caught in a bad patch, and the only remedy is to do something else.

Saying this may strain my credibility with those who are new to casino gaming, but this is the way it is. So, it is best to have an alternative on tap when it comes up. But an even better approach is to not let it come up in the first place. And the way to do that is to keep dancing from one strategy to the next, by choosing the one that looks to be the most viable for that table. This is the way I do it, and it is what I recommend for others.

Therefore, your business plan must not be one-dimensional. It has to include at least two options.

If I had to choose two gaming strategies to play forevermore, I would choose the 3Q/A and T6. Both of these yield a 2–1 return (although the T6 can be adjusted for even money). Overall, I prefer a 2–1 payoff. This is because with these two strategies, it is often easier to secure a win than with others that offer a smaller yield! So, I go where the money is.

Some players, however, may find that the wins come easier when playing a bet with a lower return, like a sledge variation, or a blend of 1–1 and 1–2 bets. Still others might be jazzed about getting a 5–1 return, which is possible with a modification of the T6: by waiting until five sixlines are hit, then targeting the sixth. And because of the high return, they might feel that an eight-bet series is justified. I've done that myself. It's doable, but I would recommend that you wait three or four spins after the trigger is identified before starting your series. This will extend your target window—but could also cause you to lose the betting opportunity. That's okay. Lots of tables out there.

Figure 48 shows a recap of the strategies offered in this book, with the page locations and bet returns. These have been arranged according to the payoffs (low to high):

STRATEGY	DESCRIBED ON PAGES	BET RETURN
SLEDGEHAMMER	93–96, 99–103, 115, 116	1–2
SLEDGE "B"	99–103	1–2
DOUBLE COLUMNS	172	1–2
T6 (1–1)	168–170	1–1
PATTERN BETS	60–65	1–1
REOCCURRING SINGLE	66–68	1–1
REOCCURRING DOUBLE	69, 70	1–1
ANGEL	97, 98, 117	2–1
3Q	104–106, 117	2–1
3Q/A	126–148	2–1
T6 (2–1)	168–170	2–1
FIXED SPLITS	118–121	5–2
T6 (5–1)	170, 227	5–1
MIXED MEDIA	122–124	VARIES
FREESTYLE	171–178	VARIES

FIGURE 48
Business Plan Strategy Options

From this list, you need to select the strategies that will form the basis of your business plan. This is the first of seven stages of the business plan: *the Selection Stage.*

Then, you need to gather table data from the roulette version (European vs. American) you expect to play. The quickest way to gather roulette statistics is with a system tester, like St. Germain's *Roulette System Tester* or Frank Scoblete's *Spin Roulette Gold.* The latter was not created as a system tester, but it happens to be the best source for gaming statistics for short sessions (like those advocated in this book) that I'm aware of. This is the second stage: *the Collection Stage.*

1) the Selection Stage (choosing a strategy)
2) the Collection Stage (collecting table data)
3) the Computation Stage (performing trials on paper)
4) the Rehearsal Stage (practice sessions)
5) the Live Trial Stage (limited, low level casino play)
6) the Evaluation Stage (analysis of that performance)
7) the Live Betting Stage (live gaming sessions)

FIGURE 49
The Stages of the Business Plan

Another way to gather table data would be to play practice sessions at an online casino, making sure, of course, to notate the table decisions as you play. Then, get several sets of copies of what you've accumulated, so you can 'crunch the numbers.'

The *Computation Stage* is where you try the chosen strategies on paper. As you do this, cover the table results you haven't gotten to yet, so you can't see what's coming. This will more effectively simulate a live gaming session.

After you have performed a few of these trials, you can start building a databank of statistics, such as wins vs. losses; longest losing streaks, etc. You might also want to try changing the series lengths, like switching from a two-stage series to three. This might enhance the performance of your strategy, or at the least, provide some new insights.

After that comes the *Rehearsal Stage,* where you act out the sessions with poker chips or the like, to synthesize the effects of live play in a casino. Now, if you plan to play online, you won't need any chips. Instead, I would recommend that you use the free play games that are available on the web.

During the *Live Trial Stage,* you want to keep your sessions very brief, and play for the lowest stakes possible. For this, I would recommend a stake of $50 for online play with $1 table minimums, or $100 for live play in a land casino. At this stage, don't try too hard to make money. What matters is how you perform when there is real money on the line.

After you have played live bets, move on to the *Evaluation Stage*. This is where you take a hard look at how your strategy did, and how *you* performed. Did you hold up okay, or do you see areas that could stand improvement? And how did the strategy perform? You may have noticed that you didn't do nearly as well during the live play as what you did on paper. That is to be expected. Paper trials are no substitute for live gaming!

The next and final stage is the *Live Betting Stage*. This is the destination to which all roads lead. But be sure you're ready for it. If you're not completely confident that you've got something that is going to kick some serious butt, you need to go back through the stages, as many times as necessary, until you feel you are as ready as you'll ever be.

Online or off, this final stage should be approached with a great deal of caution. Don't be too concerned about how much you can make. Your main objective, in fact, is to *not lose* while you put real money into action. See how long you can make a little bit of money last. If you're having difficulty, go back to the drawing board. Use your scorecards to help you find what went wrong, and why. When you think you've got the problem nailed down, go out and try it again, but with very small stakes. Before you can make money, you've got to learn the art. You've got to know the moves cold, because it's sink or swim out there.

If you find that you're making progress, don't let yourself get overconfident. There are lots of surprises around every new corner. It's just a matter of time before they catch up to you. I know this sounds a bit pessimistic, but I've lived it, and I keep living it, every day and three times on Sunday.

Your first major goal is to build a bankroll that is equivalent to the wagering fund you originally set up. If you can accomplish that, you are way ahead of what I would expect from most readers. But don't make the foolish mistake of thinking you have arrived. Having earned your first bankroll through live casino play, your new objective is to keep from losing it, while you pursue the goal of doubling it. Trust me, it's never easy. There's never a time when you can relax, and set the machine on autopilot.

GAMING PARTNERSHIPS

In my first book, *Gamble to Win,* I advised my readers that—to ensure one's success as a player—an assistant or partner was absolutely imperative. This was to separate the task into two parts: player, and treasurer. It was designed to prevent the one gambling from making foolish choices with the bankroll in the heat of battle. The treasurer was to dole out the money only as both parties had agreed to, prior to entering the casino.

This requirement was well-intentioned, but it was too much of an imposition on my readers. It was dropped, in favor of strong warnings that are offered periodically in my books. But there is no doubt in my mind that anyone who plays casino games could do so much better if they had a way to separate the *playing* aspect of the task from the *funding* aspect.

So, an imperative turns into a suggestion: if there is any way to do so, it would be to your advantage to enlist the help of a friend toward the effort of making money in a casino.

Apart from keeping the roles separate, this associate can alert you to any late-breaking news you may have missed. He can help you process the information that is constantly streaming from the table, and the casino in general. He will keep you true to your goal. He'll be your offensive and defensive coordinator, your protector, and your guardian angel.

And, when you've got company, you have a sounding board. Someone to respond to observations that would've gone unspoken, and perceptions that would not have come to light.

Making money in casinos is a tough, tough business. A little help could go a long, long way.

SUMMARY:
GETTING STARTED

If at first you don't succeed, try not to look astonished.

—from *The Cincinnati Fax News*

I've always felt that the most direct path to making money is by learning how to leverage money itself. There are many ways to do this, including stock market investing, exploiting international currency fluctuations, purchasing municipal bonds, and working in the field of finance. But it takes thousands of dollars to accomplish anything significant in these areas.

Casino gambling, when looked at as an investment, enables one to get started with less money. But the principle for leveraging income is a constant for all the above: seek small gains, until you accumulate enough capital to go for larger gains.

It sounds easy enough, but most people are used to an income situation where the money moves in only one direction. It is hard for them to face the prospect of a losing day, after all the work they put in. Some players will not respond well to these very destructive reversals of fortune. Those who succeed, do so only because they find a way to adapt to the hardship.

If you are seeking to make consistent income playing casino table games, you should know going in that the odds are strongly against you, and, that it will take an enormous amount of courage, perseverance, and determination.

Winning is not easy. Losing is not easy. If you're looking for *easy,* you won't find it here.

16

AUXILIARY ISSUES

Anyone who isn't confused doesn't really understand the situation.

—Edward R. Murrow

There is more to playing casino games than just knowing where to put your chips, and how many to lay down. There are a number of rules to observe, and restrictions to acknowledge. There is the matter of casino etiquette, and how much and when a player should tip a staff member.

Also, you should know something about how you can benefit from casino comps, since it is possible, at times, to use them as the equivalent of cash.

Then there's the matter of security. Are casinos safe? Are the towns they're in safe? And what about the games themselves? Any chance at all that they're rigged?

In the overall scheme of things, these are pretty minor issues, but they shouldn't be ignored. Since this book is being touted as having all the information you need to win in casinos, this chapter was added to address those issues.

And for those who may not know all the gaming terms, there is a glossary in the back of this book.

CASINO COMPS

Years ago, while living in L.A., I received an interesting offer in the mail. Two free weekend nights of lodging and other perks at a major casino resort in Las Vegas, if I sign up for their players card and spend some time playing at their tables. How could I refuse?

I arrived on a Friday evening, and won over $600 in a little more than two hours. Hey, I'm not seeing a downside here. After winning another $500 the next morning, I decided to spend the rest of my time there sightseeing and hanging out at the pool. They had a waterfall, water volleyball and a water slide. I must say, I thought I'd found the shortcut to heaven.

When I checked out, I was told that because of all the time I racked up at the tables, they were going to repeat the offer for a future visit. Not believing my good fortune, I said I hadn't really spent that much time playing. But they insisted that the duration of my play had thrust me into a special category.

There was no question in my mind that somebody had erred. My concern was that they would renege on their offer after I had committed myself to the five-hour trip to get there. As it turned out, their word was good. Nobody erred. They knew exactly what they were doing.

The free room, meals, and drinks I received are known as comps, or complimentaries. They are part of a methodical reward system implemented by casino management to induce players to spend more time at their tables, where it is expected they will lose. The way they see it, the cure for a player who got lucky in their casino is to entice him back to the tables.

In my case, I did not expect this ploy to work for them, since I thought I was a pretty good player. But it did work in a limited way. I lost $450 on my second trip. Knowing the exact amount of my wins and losses through my use of the players card, the casino management repeated their generous offer yet again. By that time I was starting to understand.

If you're in the habit of buying in for $200 or more at casino table games, it's only a matter of time before you're approached by a floorperson, who will encourage you to sign up for their players card, so your play can be 'rated'. Now, they use that word pretty loosely. What they really mean is 'monitored', but I guess it would be politically incorrect to use *that* word. What's really going on here is that they want to keep tabs on your gaming activity, and give you a good reason to play longer. In return, they're willing to give you free stuff.

Rating slot players – is the easiest for the casinos. The player puts his card in the credit card slot on the machine, and the internal computer automatically adds points. For table games, the process is a little more subjective. A member of casino management notes your playing time and bet levels, then has the pit bookkeeper enter the information into the house database.

The free stuff varies from one casino to the next, but for the most part it's all pretty standard. For the points you accumulate, you can get your room paid for, meals, gift items, souvenirs, travel accommodations, and sometimes even cash back.

What's the catch? In this context, *free* is just another word for *stuff that's paid for five times over at the tables.* Which means that you're expected to lose five times the value of the comps. But that's just part of the problem. When you submit to this ritual, you forfeit your low profile and your anonymity. A major concession. The last thing you need is for them to get a handle on how much money you take out of their casino each day.

And, in trying to earn comp points, you're likely to spend more time at the tables. You lose your focus.

You may be able to find a way to benefit from casino comps, but I see them as little more than a gilded snare.

TIPPING IN A CASINO

Most people who plan an overnight stay in the hotel section of a casino are recreational gamblers. They came from afar, and expect to be pampered during their visit. That's fine for them, but I never felt I could justify the expense, or afford to lose my edge by succumbing to a relaxed state.

I'm a jungle fighter, seeking only one thing: money. I'm not looking for comfort, or excitement. Therefore, I'm not an authority on tipping bellhops, valets or maitre d's. My expertise is limited to things that occur in the gaming area.

At the roulette tables, you don't see a lot of tipping going on. That's because most people lose all their chips in less than fifteen minutes, and they're a little disappointed. Tipping the dealer is not a priority for them at that point.

While I realize that the dealers have a tough job—which does not pay as well as many people think—I doubt that they expect tips from those who do nothing but lose. If someone 'hit the big one' at their table, however, I think the dealer should get a meaningful tip, as long as he was courteous and efficient.

At the craps or blackjack tables, a lot of tipping comes in the form of bets made for the dealers. But this is not so easy to do at the roulette table, because of the common playing area that exists at that game. Meaning, a tip of that kind has to be identified as such for the dealer to know what it is.

I try to give the dealer a little something (two to five bucks) from the chips he gives me, as I'm cashing out. But there are times when my heart isn't into it, because I've had a bad day.

In those situations, I think most dealers understand.

CASINO ETIQUETTE

For the most part, casino etiquette is simply a matter of being courteous and polite. If you conduct yourself as you would in an upscale restaurant, you can't go wrong.

In other words, treat the players and dealers with respect, and avoid behavior that is pushy, belligerent, or rude. If you get into a disagreement with someone, be gracious. Be the peacemaker. Be the one to back down first. Remember, a casino is your temporary place of employment, and there are twelve cameras trained on you right now, at this very moment. Whatever the problem, nothing is worth the risk or indignity of being cast as the bad guy—by anyone who may be watching.

There are, however, two rules that apply to anyone who plays roulette, which should be remembered. First, during a buy-in, don't ever attempt to hand your money to the dealer. He is not allowed to take money from your hand. Second, always wait until the dealer lifts the dolly (marking the winning number) from the table, before attempting to put down any new bets. These were covered earlier in this book, but a reminder won't hurt.

Usually, the only time etiquette becomes an issue in a casino is when a player has had too much to drink. Casinos like to project an image of being the ultimate party place, but at times a guest will take this a little too seriously. Now, if he's losing huge amounts at the tables while misbehaving, they might let him play all night! They certainly don't want to alienate the other patrons, but they're a business, and whatever brings in the top money is often what dictates the action.

Aren't all businesses like that?

SECURITY

One of the most common misconceptions of gaming that I've encountered is the notion that casinos aren't safe. Some people might suspect that casino management has notorious ties, while others are concerned for their imagined vulnerability to thieves in and around casinos.

I would guess that none of these people have recently visited Las Vegas. If they had, one glimpse of a major intersection on the strip would go a long way toward helping them see the error in their logic. We're talking families, decked out in bright Hawaiian prints, their kids in tow, who are carrying stuffed dinosaurs and sucking on lollipops. The casualness and frivolity they exude tells you in an instant that they have *no fear.*

While I will admit that I always have my guard up whenever I'm in a casino parking garage, I have never had a problem of this sort, nor have I heard of anyone else having a problem. The reason for this is that the casinos are widely known to have several levels of security, and their cameras are everywhere.

There was a time when underworld influence was keenly felt in casinos, but these days they're run by big corporations like ITT and Hilton. Their staff has to be squeaky clean because every state now has a gaming commission, and any employee having mob ties would jeopardize the casino's precious gaming license.

A little common sense is all you're likely to need to avoid being a target: dress down, don't boast about your winnings, and don't flash money around. And especially, don't go wandering the back alleys of Atlantic City at night while carrying bags of money, or wearing expensive jewelry!

RIGGED GAMES

I must insist that the cards are ill-shuffled, 'till I have a good hand.

—Swift

Most people these days realize that rigged games do not exist in the brick-and-mortar casinos. They understand that a secret like that could not be kept from 1) the dealers, who are poor working folks like most of us, and 2) the media bloodhounds, who would *love* to jump on a story like that.

In the land casinos, there is no reason for the casinos to try to rig the games, when those games are already constructed to churn out an automatic profit. And what fool of a manager would put his gaming license at risk, which typically costs six figures, and is the only thing that keeps him in business?

Ah, but when the conversation moves to online casinos, those same people have a different view. After all, how hard would it be for casino management to switch the games to manual mode, and manipulate the table results whenever some large bets are going down? What's to stop them from racking up unauthorized charges, once they get your credit card number? Cyber casinos don't have to worry about state gaming commissions, because they are located outside the United States!

These are valid concerns, which I used to share, and still do to some extent. You can only put so much trust in fictitious gaming results that are transmitted from an offshore signal, which would be outlawed if the United States government could figure out a way to stop it at the border!

It is helpful to understand how the business works. Not many people realize, for instance, that operations of the more reputable online casinos are split into three parts. The casinos don't see your credit card number because the transaction is handled by a third-party credit card processor, which forwards the money to the casino, minus the number. And they can't doctor the table results because the software is purchased from an outside company, which has encrypted the program (so it can't be altered), to protect *their* business reputation.

So, all the casino does is run the programs and make payouts to the winners. Everything else is outside their influence.

And, as noted in Chapter 13, the industry is trying to regulate itself. Organizations like the Internet Gaming Commission and the Ethical Online Gaming Association are there to listen if you had a bad experience with online gaming.

But how can a player really know nothing funny is going on, or ever will in the future? Unless you own the casino, you can't. But there are ways to protect yourself. The best way is to start out wagering small amounts, then build up your bankroll as you win. That way, most of the money at risk is *won money,* as opposed to that which was earned the hard way.

The solution offered in the paragraph above, by the way, is more than just a form of protection against online piracy. It's a prudent approach to any gaming endeavor.

If you've hit a brick wall in playing any given strategy, bear in mind that it may be attributable to statistical variance. Even the legitimate games have a way of producing some strange patterns! But to be on the safe side, bet conservatively after a fluke, and pay close attention to the new results as they unfold.

EPILOGUE

The pro knows to play by the month rather than by the day.

—David Sklansky

About ten years ago, while I was living in Las Vegas, I took a friend from California and her eight-year-old son, Ian, on a quick tour of several casinos. Minors, of course, aren't supposed to be in the gaming areas, but nobody tried to stop the three of us from "passing through." Ian was impressed with it all, particularly the ringing of the bells (which meant someone had won, I told him), and the clink of the coins (machines paying the winners, I said), but at some point, he told us that it made him sad.

"Why?" my friend and I asked, in unison.

"With all the money they're giving away, they'll be broke by the time *I'm* old enough to play!"

From the mouths of babes, comes a comment that reveals how well the casinos wear their mask of illusion.

This is what you're up against when you take on the casinos. They have the home field advantage, and they exploit it to the hilt. Because of this, your senses, instincts and expectations are misled, and your mind is sending you false signals.

To win, you've got to rise above all of that. You must not be swayed by any emotions you feel. You're a robot. An automaton. A cold, unfeeling monolith that performs a mechanical function, dutifully and reliably. You don't see a thing, hear a thing, smell a thing, feel a thing.

The best way to do this is to keep your sessions brief and stay focused on your goal. Pretend you're wearing blinders if you must. Remember why you came: to make some money. You didn't come to see the fake Elvis, or impress the girls with the size of your bets, or fill up on the free drinks. You're at your place of employment, and you've got a job to do.

Keeping yourself detached from all the manipulative devices out there is never easy. Especially, when one considers the duality of the casino: it is your adversary, but it is also the closest thing you have to an employer. Thus, you have to be comfortable with the notion that *your opponent is feeding you.* You need to defeat him, but you also need him to stay solvent, so you can do it again tomorrow. You can never really achieve full victory, for that would deprive you of your income source!

One of the biggest mistakes made by aspiring professionals is to try to recoup losses immediately. When they suffer a bad loss, they are obsessed with a need to get even. So, they start playing wildly in a desperate attempt to win back what they lost. But that only compounds the damage.

A real pro doesn't try too hard to get even for the day. Sure, he'd like to see that happen, but he knows that he has no choice but to take what the table gives him. Trying to force a win won't help. What will be, will be. To him, all wins and losses are just part of an endless chain of numbers. He knows that all he has to do is keep playing his game, same as always, and the wins will come around. There is no need to press the issue.

Just like a banker or financier, your job is to squeeze out a profit from the money that flows through the system. You capture whatever amounts you can, by reaping the bounty of the seeds you plant. But you never know which seed is going to grow. You can't yell *"Grow, dammit!"* to the seed, and expect that to work. You've got to be patient, and let it happen naturally.

The way to win is to *tailor your play to the results the table is disposed to give.* That's all you gotta do. Just keep thinking that, and you'll get there.

Stay focused. Dance the dance. Gamble to Win.

SCORECARD PLATES

Figures 50 and 51 on the following two pages are scorecard plates, which were added to enable readers to get scorecards of their own printed up. Figure 50 can be printed two different ways: two-up on a sheet, then trimmed and bound into pads of fifty sheets apiece. These are for live casino play in a brick-and-mortar casino. The other way is four-up on a letter-size sheet, which can be copied in that state, to be used for online wagering. Any copy place like Kinko's or Alphagraphics can handle either order if you provide them with this book (to create the new originals), and the instructions as specified in Chapter 12.

Those two pages, by the way, are the only exceptions to the copyright restriction that applies to the rest of this book.

If you wish to order a specialty scorecard, designed to your specifications, you may contact me through my email address at rdellison2002@yahoo.com. Since my email addresses have been known to change, however, try my website at gamble2win.com if you have difficulty getting through. My current email address should be listed somewhere at that site.

The price for an original laser print of a specialty scorecard is $25, provided that the instructions are reasonably clear. Changes to a design are $15, as long as they are not extensive. Otherwise, the $25 charge will apply, again.

There is no postage charge, but be sure to provide complete contact information.

Also, any readers who have questions about any content in this book may contact me via the above.

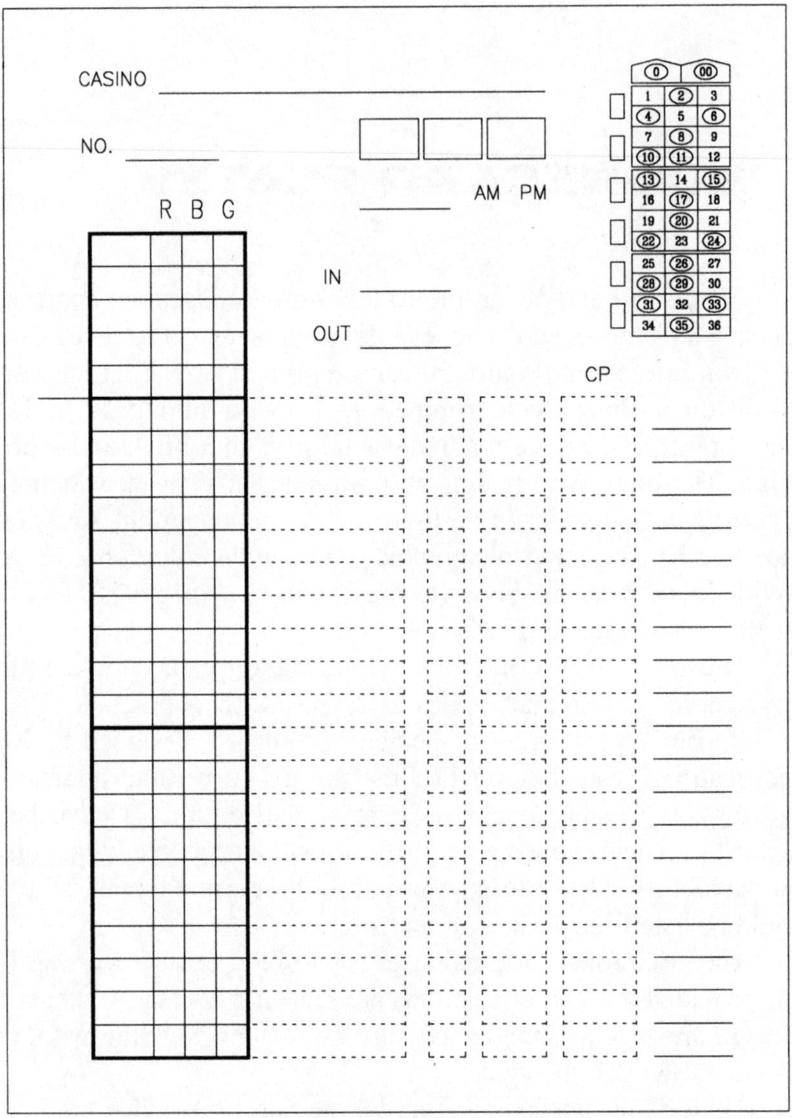

CASINO _____

NO. _____ 　　　[ ] [ ] [ ]

　　　　　　　　　　　　　　_____ AM PM

R B G

IN _____

OUT _____

CP

FIGURE 50
The Roulette Scorecard

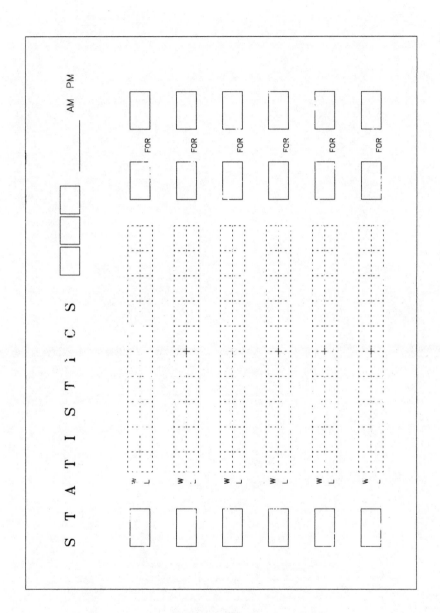

FIGURE 51
The Statistics Scorecard

GLOSSARY
OF ROULETTE AND GENERAL
GAMING TERMS

Ace-Deuce A craps term for the number 3 on a pair of dice.

Aces A craps term for the number 2 on a pair of dice.

Action Betting activity, usually in a casino.

Advantage See *House Edge.*

American Roulette One of several roulette versions, characterized by two green numbers, the 0 and 00.

Angel Defined in this book as a two-unit *inside* roulette bet that covers the 1–6 and 31–36 sixlines.

Anti-Martingale The opposite of the *Martingale* system in gaming, involving the doubling of one's bet size after winning, as opposed to doubling the bet size after a loss.

Atlantic City roulette A variation of American roulette that has a special rule which benefits the player: when a 0 or 00 wins, the dealer returns half of any *outside* even money bet (as opposed to the bet being an outright loss).

Automaton A robot; a being that behaves in an automatic or mechanical fashion.

Auxiliary Bet Referred to in this book as a wager that falls outside the scope of the primary wagering strategy, but is used to exploit a conspicuous table condition.

Baccarat A casino table game, played with several decks of cards that are dealt from a shoe.

Bank One of the two main wagering options at the game of baccarat and minibaccarat. Also called *Banker.*

Bank Craps The game of *Craps,* where players bet against the house, instead of each other.

Banker A synonym of *Bank.*

Bankroll Sometimes called a *stake,* this term applies to the amount of money one has set aside specifically for the purpose of placing bets at games of chance.

Bareback Betting without the accompaniment of a hedge bet, as protection against losing to a longshot.

Bet A wager. Any amount of money used for a speculative investment at a game of chance.

Bet the Farm To risk a considerable sum of money, likely to overextend the player in the event of a loss.

Betting Strategy A technique employed by a bettor which aspires to bring financial gain.

Betting Trigger See *Trigger.*

Bettor One who places wagers or bets.

Big One An insider casino term for $1000.

Bill An insider casino term for a $100 bill.

Black 1) A roulette bet that pays even money, opposite to the even money bet *Red.* 2) A $100 gaming token, which is issued, and used as money, in a casino.

Blackjack 1) A table game played with one to eight decks of cards. 2) An original hand of a ten and an ace, or a face card and an ace, at the game of *blackjack.*

Blacks Casino gaming chips or tokens having a face value of $100 within the gaming area of the issuing casino, so called because of their color, black.

Brick-and-Mortar Casino A conventional casino, built on real estate, as opposed to an online casino, which exists strictly in cyberspace. Also referred to in this book as a *land-based* casino, or, simply, a *land* casino.

Buy-In The monetary figure exchanged for casino chips at the commencement of table game wagering.

Cashier One who handles monetary transactions in a casino, such as exchanging gaming tokens for cash, or processing payments for cash advances or markers.

Cashier Cage The area where the *casino cashier* works, so called because of the bars or glass partition that customarily separate the cashier from the public.

Casino 1) A building, or area within a building, where games of chance are offered to the public. 2) A term indicating the *house,* the entity players bet against.

Casino Manager The executive in charge of all operations within a casino.

Change Color To convert casino gaming chips to larger or smaller denomination chips.

Chart 1) To analyze the results or numerical patterns that accrue at a casino table game. 2) To document those results on a sheet of paper, for immediate or later use.

Check A casino gaming chip or token.

Chemin De Fer A variation of baccarat, where the players bet against each other, rather than against the house.

Chip A gaming token, used as money in a casino.

Closed Progression A series of bets that increase in size as losses continue, until the fixed upward limit is reached.

"Color" A term used by some players to alert the dealer that they are leaving the table, and wish to have their *colored* chips exchanged for *value* chips.

"Color In" An expression dealers use to notify a superior that a player is leaving the table, and his chips are being converted to *value chips,* or higher denomination chips.

Colored Chips Tokens used at a roulette table that may not leave the table, and must be exchanged for *value* chips before the player departs. Also called *table chips* or *house chips.*

Column Bet A roulette *outside* bet that covers a column of twelve specific numbers, and pays 2–1. There are three such bet options at any roulette version.

Comfort Zone The range of bet levels at which the player feels comfortable with the monetary risk involved.

Commission A fee charged by casinos for selected wagers, in lieu of the *house edge.*

Comp See *Complimentary.*

Complimentary A signed ticket that entitles the player to free meals, lodging, or the like. Offered by casinos as a reward for playing time accrued at the tables.

Compression Principle *For every absence of a probable event, there is an equivalent compression of subsequent events.* See Chapter 3.

Compulsion Defined in this book as the inherent part of human nature to become reckless or irrational with one's money in certain gaming situations.

Continuum Defined in this book as the ongoing sequence of betting opportunities in casinos, giving players insufficient time to make intelligent betting decisions.

Contra D'Alembert The inverse of the *D'Alembert* system for even money wagers. See Chapter 8.

Controlled Greed Defined in this book as the paradoxical attitude that can enhance one's chances for success at the tables: *a passionate desire for a sensible bet acquisition.*

Corner Bet A roulette inside bet covering four contiguous numbers on the layout, which pays 8–1. So called because a chip representing the bet is placed at the intersecting corners of the four. Also referred to as a *quad* bet.

CP An abbreviation used in this book, which stands for *Cumulative Profit.*

Craps 1) A table game played with a pair of dice. 2) A dice roll of 2, 3 or 12 at the game of craps, which causes a loss to all *pass line* bets when rolled during the come-out.

Crew Casino personnel who staff a craps table.

Croupier A dealer of roulette or baccarat.

Customized Scorecard A card for charting table results, which has been designed specifically for that need. See Chapter 12, and pages 243 through 245.

D'Alembert System A technique designed for even-money wagers that calls for bet fluctuations at predetermined intervals. Also called the *Pyramid.*

Dealer The casino staff member who runs a table game or assists in its execution.

Deck A group of 52 playing cards, used for table games such as baccarat, blackjack and poker.

Deuce The number 2, at cards or dice.

Dice A pair of six-sided cubes, marked on all sides with dots representing numbers, used at craps and other games.

Die The singular of *Dice*.

Dollar A casino term for a $1 or $100 gaming token.

Dominant Trend A trend that favors a certain category of results at a casino table game.

Double Street A roulette wager that covers six contiguous numbers on the layout. Also called a *Sixline*.

Double Zero One of the two green numbers (0 and 00) that represent a gaming result at American roulette.

Downside A disadvantageous aspect or occurrence.

Dozens Bet At roulette, one of three wagers that pay 2–1: *1st Dozen* (numbers 1–12), *2nd Dozen* (numbers 13–24), or *3rd Dozen* (numbers 25–36).

Dry Bet An imaginary bet, made to postulate a theoretical result at a game of chance.

Edge See *House Edge*.

Encompassing Trend The sum of all the minor table trends occurring at a casino table game; the overall inclination of a table to favor a wagering result.

En Prison A feature of European roulette, where all even money bets are impounded by the dealer—when 0 is the result—pending the result of the next *non-zero* spin.

European Roulette A version of roulette, characterized by a single green number (0), as opposed to two, or three.

Even One of six *outside* roulette bets that pay even money, opposite to the even money bet *odd*.

Even Money A bet return that pays 1–1.

Face Card A Jack, Queen or King from a deck of cards, having a value of 10 at blackjack, and 0 at baccarat.

Favorite A term used in competitions and gambling, which indicates the probable winner *in the opinion of* the oddsmaker and/or the public in general.

Fiveline An *inside* bet at American roulette that covers the five numbers at the top of the layout: 0, 00, 1, 2 and 3. This carries the highest vigorish (7.89%) of any roulette bet.

Fixed Splits Defined in this book as a collection of five split bets that cover a fixed group of roulette numbers.

Flat Bets A term used in this book that indicates a string of bets that do not fluctuate in size.

Floorperson A roving troubleshooter who supervises all the games in a designated area of a casino.

Gambler One who puts money at risk for speculative gain, either as a recreational pastime or as a vocation.

Gambling The act of risking money at games of chance, or any other speculative venture.

Gaming Associated with gambling.

Gaming Commission A state regulatory agency that is responsible for licensing casinos, monitoring the cash flow in casinos, and fielding customer inquiries.

Gaming Specialist A professional gambler who specializes in certain casino table games.

Generic Chips Gaming chips or tokens that can be used at any table game in the casino, as opposed to *colored chips,* which may not leave the table. Also called *value chips.*

Greens Value chips that are used for table game play, which have a face value of $25. Also called *quarters.*

Grind What one must endure to succeed as a professional gambler!

Handicapper One who analyzes performance statistics in an effort to choose the probable winner of a race or contest.

Hedge See *Hedge Bet.*

Hedge Bet An additional bet, smaller than one's primary bet but paying higher odds, designed to protect the bettor against a loss attributed to a longshot.

Hedge Bettor One who advocates and plays *hedge bets* in an attempt to mitigate the potential downside.

High An even money roulette bet that covers the numbers 19–36, opposite to the bet *Low,* which covers 1–18.

High Roller One who frequently places large bets.

Horseplayer In this book, the term is meant to apply to those who bet on horses at thoroughbred racetracks.

Horseplaying Speculating (betting) on racehorses, at racetracks or offtrack betting parlors.

House A casino; the entity players bet against.

House Advantage See *House Edge*.

House Chips Another name for the *colored chips,* or *table chips,* that are used exclusively for roulette.

House Edge The statistical advantage enjoyed by casinos, derived by paying off winning bets at a rate below the amount that would equitably compensate the risk involved. Also referred to as *Advantage, House Advantage, Vigorish* and *Vig*.

Inside Bet At roulette, a wager made on an *inside* number or group of *inside* numbers on the layout.   .

Inside Number At American roulette, one of 38 numbers that appear in the main area of the layout, where chips representing wagers are placed. (At European roulette, there are just 37 numbers instead of 38.)

Intercasino An online casino, where live casino gambling and practice games are offered to the public. The website address is www.intercasino.com. Considered by the author of this book to be one of the more reputable, and therefore safer, cybercasinos in existence at the time of this writing.

Junket A chartered trip to a casino that is priced below the market value, because participants are expected or required to spend time gambling (and therefore, losing).

Keno A casino game that is similar to a state lottery, in that it offers the potential for a large return from a small investment, but which carries an abnormally high *house edge*.

Labouchère A system for even money bets that involves a notation procedure to establish the bet size.

Land-based Casino See *Brick-and-Mortar Casino*.

Land Casino See *Brick-and-Mortar Casino*.

Layout The printed felt or material that represents the area where bets are placed at a casino table game.

Let It Ride 1) To add the proceeds of a winning bet to the original wager, to fashion a new, larger bet. Also called a *parlay*. 2) A casino table game of that name.

Longshot A bet that statistically has a small chance to win, but offers the potential for a high return.

Longshot Specialist One who specializes in playing bets that carry a high payoff relative to the bet size.

Loss Limit A monetary boundary, applied to a bankroll, which is designed to protect the player from making impulsive or regrettable wagering choices.

Lotto A bet option at state lotteries that offers a huge return from a $1 wager (but is not realistically attainable).

Low An even money roulette bet that covers the numbers 1–18, opposite to the bet *high,* which covers 19–36.

Martingale A system, usually applied to even money bets, which involves doubling one's bet size with each loss, as often as necessary, in an attempt to recoup previous losses.

MiniBaccarat A scaled-down version of baccarat, which moves faster and is less formal.

Mini-Martingale A variation of the *Martingale* system, which calls for one to abandon the series and write off that loss if a win is not produced from one of its three stages.

Mixed Media A selection of even money bets, designed to hold one's seat at a table game while awaiting a betting opportunity for another procedure. See Chapter 10.

Money Wheel A casino game where a large circular disk— with currency placed on its face in a circular pattern—is spun by a dealer to arrive at a decision.

Monkey A slang expression for a face card, sometimes heard at blackjack, baccarat or minibaccarat tables.

Multiple-Deck Shoe A device used by dealers to dispense playing cards for blackjack, baccarat and minibaccarat.

Multiple Parlay A parlay that exceeds one stage.

Natural 1) At the casino table game craps, a roll of 7 or 11 during the come-out. 2) At minibaccarat, an original hand with a point value of 8 or 9.

Negative Trend Defined in this book as *the conspicuous absence of a gaming event.* See Chapter 3.

Nickel A gaming token having a face value of $5, used for placing bets. Also called a *Red.*

Odd A roulette *outside* bet that pays even money, opposite to the bet called *Even.*

Odds 1) The statistical probability for an event to occur; often applied to casino games. 2) A term sometimes used to mean the *house edge.*

Odds-on A bet that returns less than even money, usually associated with racetrack wagering.

1–2–3–4 System A closed progression comprised of four bets that increase in size after each loss, until the ceiling is reached or a win occurs. See Chapter 8.

Oscar's Grind One of the more effective systems for even money bets known to gamblers. See Chapter 8.

Outside Bet A roulette wager played in an area adjacent, but not within, the area of the layout numbers. All *outside* wagers pay either 1–1 or 2–1.

Overview A card-counting procedure for blackjack, which is easier to execute than conventional card counting, since it does not involve mathematics that are as precise.

Parlay 1) A bet comprised of its original amount, plus its winnings, forming a new, larger bet. 2) To place such a bet.

Paroli 1) A near-obsolete term for parlay. 2) A new, larger bet that is formed from a parlayed wager, *plus* the addition of an amount equaling that of the original bet.

Past-Posting The (illegal) act of placing or increasing a bet after the wagering result is known.

Payoff The return on a successful bet.

Percentage A term sometimes used to mean *House Edge.*

Pit An area of a casino surrounded by gaming tables.

Pit Boss The casino executive in charge of the pit.

Player 1) One who risks money at games of chance, such as those offered in a casino. 2) The name of one of the two primary betting options at baccarat and minibaccarat.

Point Spread The number of points added to the underdog point total in a sports bet, which the favorite must overcome for a bet on the favorite to win.

Poker A card game, found in casinos, which has several variations.

Positive Trend Defined in this book as the *presence* of a conspicuous trend or gaming event. See Chapter 3.

Press 1) To increase the size of a wager, often using the proceeds of a successful bet to do so. 2) The verbal command to a dealer to increase the size of one's bet.

Press and Pull A technique for fluctuating the size of bets, advocated in this book. See Chapter 5.

Press It Up A verbal command to a dealer, particularly at the game of craps, to increase the size of a bet.

Professional A term used in this book, meant to describe those who gamble professionally.

Professional Gambler One whose primary source of income is derived from gambling.

Profit The amount that is won from a single wager, or an amount won over a period of time.

Progression A series of bets that increase in size until a win occurs, or the end of the wagering cycle is reached, at which time a new series may begin.

Push 1) A tie, at a table game such as blackjack, craps or minibaccarat. 2) The act of achieving a tie, as noted above.

Quad A bet at roulette, which covers four (contiguous) *inside* numbers. Also called a *Corner Bet.*

Quarter A *generic* gaming chip having a face value of $25, used for table game play in casinos. Also called a *Green.*

Racetrack In this book, the term is meant to apply only to thoroughbred racetracks.

Reality Check A procedure for monitoring one's behavior in a casino, advocated in this book, as a supplement to one's *loss limits* and *win goals.* See Chapter 7.

Recreational Gambler One who gambles for recreation or sport, relying primarily on luck to win.

Red 1) A roulette *outside* bet paying even money, opposite to the even money bet *black*. 2) A $5 gaming chip, used for table game play. Also called a *Nickel*.

Regression A bet that is smaller in amount than a previous (successful) wager.

Reoccurring Double Defined in this book as an even money trend where one or both of the primary wagering options manifest a pattern of consecutive wins. See Chapter 6.

Reoccurring Single Defined in this book as an even money trend where one of the primary wagering options shows a pattern of isolated wins amidst a multitude of wins from the opposing side. See Chapter 6.

Roulette A table game, invented in France, which uses a small ball set loose inside a revolving wheel to produce an official result. See Chapter 4.

Roulette Layout The felt-lined table top that has imprinted boxes and numbers, representing the areas reserved for wagering at the game of roulette. See Chapter 4.

Roulette Wheel A device used to produce the winning numbers for roulette, which spins in one direction while a small ball is set in motion in the other direction, until coming to rest in a numbered slot. See Chapter 4.

Sands of the Caribbean An online casino where live casino gambling and practice games are offered. Their website address is www.thesands.com. Considered by the author to be one of the more reputable, and therefore safer, cybercasinos in existence at the time of this writing.

Scared Money Money put at risk by a player that is part of a fund insufficient for the task.

Scorecard A card or piece of paper used to chart gaming results, as a means of identifying current trends at that table. Available upon request at roulette and minibaccarat tables in most major casinos.

Scoresign Defined in this book as the lighted sign adjacent to roulette tables (in many casinos), which reveals the last fifteen or more decisions at that table.

Seated Player A player at a table game such as roulette or minibaccarat, who is more or less compelled to venture a wager with every decision, or forfeit his seat.

Series A betting progression or group of bets that complete a wagering cycle.

Session 1) The period of time a player spends placing bets at a casino table game. 2) The duration of a riverboat cruise, where live gaming is offered to the passengers.

Settle for 90 Described in this book as sound wagering advice: *don't obsess over the need to win an arbitrary amount; take what comes and be thankful it wasn't a loss.*

Seven of Nine A repatriated human, formerly a *Borg.*

Shift Boss The executive in charge of all operations within the casino during his work shift.

Shill One hired by a casino to play table games, as a means of attracting (legitimate) players to the game.

Shoe A device used for dispensing playing cards at table games such as blackjack, baccarat and minibaccarat.

Singles The term for $1 gaming chips. Also referred to as *whites* in many casinos.

Sixline An *inside* bet for roulette covering six contiguous numbers and paying 5–1. See Chapter 4.

Sledgehammer A four-unit *inside* roulette bet that covers 24 numbers and pays 1–2. See Chapter 9.

Split Bet An *inside* roulette bet that covers 2 numbers and pays 17–1. See Chapter 4.

Sports Betting A wagering option that is available online and in Nevada casinos, which allows one to wager on publicized sports events and contests.

Stake Money risked on a wager, or the bankroll used to finance that activity.

Statistical Casino Advantage See *House Edge.*

Straight Up The term commonly used for a bet on a single *inside* number at roulette. See Chapter 4.

Streak 1) A string of consecutive gaming decisions of the same result. 2) A string of consecutive wins or losses.

Street An *inside* roulette bet that covers three numbers in a row on the layout. Also called a *Threeline.*

Strike Another term for *Surgical Strike.*

Surgical Strike Defined in this book as a single wager or limited wagering series, placed at random at a casino table game. See Chapter 10.

System A structured wagering procedure that aspires to outperform random wagering.

Table Game Any one of several games offered in a casino, including *roulette, craps, minibaccarat* and *blackjack.*

Table Limit Another term for *Table Maximum.*

Table Maximum The maximum figure allowed for bets at a casino table game, usually noted on a small placard near the dealer.

Table Minimum The minimum figure allowed for a bet or group of bets at a table game.

Table Trend A conspicuous pattern of results occurring at a casino table game.

Takeout In horse racing, the slice the racetrack takes out of the wagering pool to pay itself. Also called *juice.*

31 System One of several gaming systems described in this book, which has a betting cycle that costs 31 units.

Threeline Bet See *Street.*

Tie A secondary bet option at baccarat and minibaccarat that pays 8–1 and carries a *vigorish* of 14.1%.

Toke A tip to a dealer or casino employee.

Token Another name for gaming chip, though commonly associated with the metal type used in slot machines.

Trend A general tendency or inclination.

Trial An example or attempt.

Trigger A gaming result that serves as the signal to place a bet or commence a wagering progression.

Twenty-One (21) Another name for *Blackjack.*

Upside An advantageous aspect or occurrence.

Value Chips Gaming chips or tokens that can be used at any table game in the casino. Also called *generic chips.*

Vig An abbreviation for *Vigorish.*

Vigorish See *House Edge.*

Waddlers Obese, slow-moving casino patrons whose only purpose in life is, or seems to be, to obstruct casino foot traffic.

Wager A bet; money put at risk at a game of chance.

Wagering Mandate Defined in this book as the obligation to continue betting, or risk forfeiture of one's seat at a table game. See Chapter 5.

Wagering Trigger See *Trigger.*

Whale An insider's term for a *high roller* who is inclined to risk huge sums of money playing casino games.

White A $1 gaming chip, also called a *single.* Note: some casinos use a color other than white for their $1 chips, in which case the term may not apply.

Win 1) To profit from a successful wager. 2) A successful wager, series, session, or day.

Win Goal A predetermined monetary goal set by serious players, at which point no more money, or a sharply reduced amount, is put at risk.

Zero 1) One of two green numbers (0 and 00) that represent wagering options at American roulette. 2) At European roulette, the only green number.